Letters from
CLOTILDE

Letters from
CLOTILDE

Her life in Paris, 1891–1942

Lydie Haenlin

THE CRICKET PUBLISHER OF AURORA

AURORA, NEW YORK

Published by
The Cricket Publisher of Aurora
261 Main Street, Aurora, NY 13026

Cover photo: *Rainy day in Paris,* 1934, Brassaï

ISBN-10: 1-7923-2396-4
ISBN 13: 978-1-7923-2396-6

For Mireille

who shares Clotilde's love for the arts and fabrics

Contents

Introduction   ix

Chapter 1   *Building One's Life*   1

Chapter 2   *An Unexpected Love Life*   47

Chapter 3   *Another Self*   115

Endnotes   178

Renowned people and companies
    mentioned in the Letters   179

Acknowledgments   185

⁓

Introduction

SINCE my early childhood, the name Clotilde has been
synonymous with charm, elegance, many talents and,
above all, kindness. The woman whose name it was, guided
and inspired my mother, her niece. Clotilde was the artist who
gave her a deep respect for the arts, a true desire for beauty,
a lasting pleasure in painting. She was the seamstress who
transmitted to my mother her love for fabrics and fashion.

She was as well the one who reinforced in her niece the wish
to run her own life, to not count on others to reach her goals.
For all of us, she was strong yet sweet; she was the loving and
deeply loved woman we all wanted to be.

Thanks to a scrapbook, some letters, post-cards and
objects kept by my mother, as well as genealogical research, I
discovered many facts which enlightened us on the origins and
destiny of this beloved Clotilde.

Born in 1872, in Paris, rue du Faubourg Saint Antoine,
Clotilde Loeven showed a true talent in the arts (drawing
and classical music) and fashion. Her work in these fields was
neither easy nor expected in her social milieu, which included
mostly craftsmen and civil servants. Indeed, the Loevens,
originally from the Netherlands, had been cabinetmakers

for four generations in this working class section of Paris. Following the decline of cabinetmaking, they went into piano making around 1850, then they left the Faubourg to join the Erard Company, rue de Flandre, in the North-East of Paris, just after the Franco-Prussian war of 1870.

It is interesting to add that Jean-Louis Loeven, the half-Jewish Dutch great-grandfather who came to Paris, married the daughter of a fellow craftsman, a Catholic Parisian, around 1769, soon after his arrival. His integration in this renowned Faubourg was easy and fast. His male descendants all married catholic women from the same milieu. Most of those women were born in the countryside (Orléanais, Touraine, Nord Pas-de-Calais) but were then raised in Paris where their parents settled as craftsmen or shopkeepers. Clotilde's father took another path: His wife belonged to the lower nobility of the Artois and the provincial financial and military administrators. Furthermore, the philosophic movements of the century influenced as well and durably thoughts and life style of these Artesians. This explains the choices that shaped the destiny of Clotilde nestled in the heart of an extended family and in social relations somewhat surprising.

The Loeven children were all sent to school and knew how to read and write before it was required by law in1881. By age thirteen, the boys learned their fathers' trades, and the girls that of their mothers. Clotilde and her brother, Edouard, followed suit. Edouard became a cabinetmaker and woodcarver like his father, Jean-Baptiste Loeven. Clotilde learned to sew at her mother's side, as was expected; but she did go further along.

෬෬

The letters in this book cover three stages of Clotilde's life: a young woman full of hopes, a free, determined adult, and a wise, elderly lady. They are addressed to Eugénie, her best friend; to her cousin, Auguste, and his parents; to her great-uncle, Louis Rouyer; to a longtime friend and mentor, Alfred de Berlantie; to her lover, Jean-Louis Leroy; to her sister-in-law, Angèle, and her niece, Jacqueline; and finally to a long-time family friend, Louis Renault.

The letters allow us to understand Clotilde's thinking and expectations, as well as her surroundings. They reveal the life of the young woman both sentimental and independent, as well as her point of view concerning the important events of her time, the women's role, and the limits imposed on them. They tell what had been beneficial for the aging lady and what gave a sense to her remarkable destiny as well as what she missed.

A few photographs, kept devoutly by her niece, illustrate the charm and attractive personality of this endearing lady.

The many postcards sent to Jacqueline (who collected them diligently according to the widespread trend in France, between the two World Wars) illustrate Clotilde's deep desire to satisfy her niece's interests, but also to guide her, to participate actively in her education.

Members of the Guyot family, mentioned in Clotilde's letters

Auguste Alexis Guyot 1797–1875   +1820

Joséphine	Clotilde Scolastique	Candide Charles
1821–1892	1822–1872	1825–1910
+1837	+	+1857
Pierre Lagazy	Edouard Robin	Virginie Brécion
1815–1887	1818–1844	1836–1866
xxxx–xxxx	Maria	Charles Ernest
	1843–1917	1857–19xx
	+1865	
	Jean Baptiste Loeven	
	1842–1922	

Edouard	**Clotilde**
1866–1924	1872–1942
+1917	
Angèle Schmit	
1885–1963	
Jacqueline	
1914–2009	

+ followed by a date undicates a marriage

Clotilde's letters are addressed to the people whose names are in bold.

Bénédicte Ansart de Bofle et de Marcon 1797–1881

|

| | |

Jeanne Émilie
1829–1886

+1848

Louis Cousin
181x–1859

|

Candide
1848–1907

+1859

Ernest Delalleau
1836–1928

+1865

Louis Rouyer
1819–1905

Sara Caroline
1830–1893

+   +1869

inconnu   Jules Boucher d'Argis
18xx–1848   1814–1882

| |

Alexandre   Alphonse Jules 1856–1932
1848–1920   Jules Charles 1861–1929

+1876   Henri Gaspard 1864–1896

Rose Lacaille   Paul Louis 1871–1915
1836–1928

|

Auguste Emmanuel Guyot
1875-1941

+1916   +1938

Marie Delpierre   Madeleine Michot
1887–1968   1895–197X

|

Robert
1931–1996

+ without a date indicates a relationship not recognized officially

Clotilde at 20, in the photograph gifted by her uncle.

Chapter 1
Building One's Life

Letters from July 1891 to October 1892 sent to

Eugénie, her best friend

Alfred de Berlantier, her friend and mentor

Auguste Guyot, her cousin

Louis Rouyer, her grand-uncle

My dear Eugénie,

I am so happy to learn from your grandmother that you have settled in Arras without difficulty and that you appreciate your classy city home — a big step has been taken. But how strange it is to find myself so far from you; I miss our conversations so much! I do not doubt that you feel the same way. So we must use our pens! I hope that you share with me this urge to write and feel a real pleasure in reading my letters . . .

So, tell me very soon what you have done and discovered since your departure last Monday. I do not have much to say on my side, and certainly of no great interest. However a question my mother mumbled this morning ("who knows what awaits us?") brought back to mind a topic we discussed at length over the last few months: our choices of a profession, of a husband.

Yes, our choices. In fact, do we have any choice? Can we in any way influence our fate? You are, as I am, far from thinking so. For instance, I can still hear your voice, during our farewell dinner, when you said to your parents: "That is all well and good, but what kind of future do I have now that we are leaving Paris for the countryside?" You had such a melancholic look! And the kindly smile of your father did not seem to reassure you, nor did his vague and expected answer: "We have plenty of time to think about that; for now, we must build relationships, get used to a new way of life." Little does he think about your desires, your aspirations, your needs. For him, what is important is to marry you to some local dignitary, some bourgeois . . .

Oh, my friend, I do understand your anxiety because your

parents expect you, as a docile daughter, to take the beaten path, to become a submissive and caring wife. But then, what will happen to your art, the pleasure, the joy you find in singing?

Our parents love us and want what they call "happiness" for us, but they never question the legitimacy of their choices as far as we are concerned. We cannot escape their habit of keeping us on a leash, in spite of our education and talents. And all this is due to the need for us to occupy the place imposed by our traditional and patriarchal society! Here I am mostly thinking of you, for my mother is without any doubt more accommodating than your father. I must say that she comes from a rather rebellious family, and she tends to listen to those around her; this is a godsend for Edouard and me! In short I shall say that I am a bit heard; but, alas, that is not the case for you.

But you must NOT forget your dreams! Yes, you must absolutely keep on singing: you are so talented! Your soprano voice is so ravishing! Your mother shares my admiration of your talents; she will, without any doubt, support you when you decide to work with a good voice instructor. I am sure there should be a few in Arras. And I believe that the Conservatory in Lille has a great reputation. You could certainly get in: they just have to hear you . . . I often imagine us on stage: you the magnificent soprano and me accompanying you on my harp! Yes, I know for sure that you could easily become the next Emma Calvé, or, if you prefer, Rose Caron!

I may be exaggerating a little bit, but it never hurts to have dreams, to go beyond what is close at hand, as Sister Pauline used to say (I often think of her). Oh, my dear, dear Eugénie, how those years of study and reflection have changed us; how much I miss all of that!

But let us get back to your future as a soprano; I just thought of a possible option: in one way you are lucky to be in Arras, since my cousins, the Ansarts and the Jesuprets, are so well known there, above all in the art world. I am sure they would be happy to introduce you to a chapel master or whoever could help you. As you know, a solid introduction is still today more effective than any diploma . . . and these very accommodating cousins will be more than happy to help out the very best friend of their favorite cousin, above all when they see how charming, how pretty, how talented you are! I am going to write to them this evening, I will be your most efficient "go between."

I have to go now to deliver a dress that Mother just finished repairing. It belongs to an elderly lady in the rue Crozatier. Yes, I serve as a gopher while waiting to become a "midinette" — or should I say "cousette," "petite-main?" There are so many somewhat condescending words to call a young seamstress!

I will post my letter before the evening mail collection. But write soon to keep up our "conversation" and assure me that you are working on your voice and repertoire while waiting to work under the direction of a very qualified instructor!

I am awaiting your letter with the utmost
impatience and sending tender hugs and kisses.
CLOTILDE

MONDAY, AUGUST 4, 1891

My dear Eugénie,

Your letter arrived this morning as you were hoping. I hasten therefore to reply so that you can read my letter before the end of the week, and miss me less, perhaps? I simply cannot believe that we have been apart for only sixteen days — in what condition will we be when you come to visit me in December? For you will come, right? Promise me! Swear to it!

One thought comes to me that might render your absence acceptable: imagine talking to each other at a distance! Imagine what a joy it would be to each have in our hallway a telephone! Yes, a telephone, this magic object that everyone would like to possess, that fabulous instrument that testifies to the creativity, the incredible ingenuity of man . . . Imagine the conversations we could have now that Arras is linked to Paris! Imagine, imagine! But what good is it to dream, knowing that an annual subscription costs 200 francs (according to my brother) — and I do not know a single person in the Faubourg who owns this rare object. Even my cousin d'Argis does not have one in his lovely manor in the rue du Ranelagh! What is more, those who do have one are not really among our friends, at least for the time being. We will have to be content with our letters until you return.

But let us speak of the news you sent me. I am so happy to know that you were able to convince your parents of the necessity of taking singing lessons again. In addition, my cousins, who already answered me, will be happy to help you find the very best person to guide you to glory. No, I am not exaggerating, I am simply aware of your talents!

I am also delighted to hear that you appreciate the warm welcome of your neighbors. It is not surprising that the members of our loyal administration respect and seek each other out. But I also pray that your father does not find too soon, among his young colleagues and neighbors, the "perfect" husband for his darling daughter.

Since you mention Edouard, I must admit that I, too, had hoped that you would find him to your taste, for you often told me that you found him handsome, pleasant and sensitive, and that he impressed you with his height, his quick wit and his talent as a dancer. Nonetheless, my brother does not belong to your world: a cabinet-maker, as talented as he may be, cannot compete with the bourgeois friends of your family. What is more, with cabinetry in our Faubourg having lost its wind, Edouard's earnings are not high, and the little studio he lives in is hardly sufficient to accommodate a young family. Be that as it may, it is clear to me that your parents will attempt to find for you the most suitable husband. So draw them a convincing portrait of the man of your dreams, the one you describe me so often, and who so resembles mine: handsome if possible, assuredly elegant, certainly attentive, intelligent goes without saying, and able to respect the independent mind of women. The perfect man as it were.

Concerning my professional activities, as you so prettily call them, they are always as varied, but hardly better defined. I am discovering, little by little, under the strict guidance of my mother, what pleases and displeases me in the profession of a seamstress. I will speak of it in greater detail in my next letter, for I need to go and purchase some braid (fabric-tape in fact) and want to mail this letter on my way so you can get it before Saturday. However, rest assured: I take time every day to practice my harp; and pencils and drawing paper are always at hand! You will be able to judge my progress upon your return to our wonderful capital.

> *I send you all my love,*
> Your Clo

♋

TUESDAY, AUGUST 11, 1891

My dear, dear Friend,

I am delighted to learn that you appreciate my letters, since it is a real pleasure for me to share my ideas and my ramblings with you. Sister Theresa was right to call us the "philosophers." I miss her too, so much!

As for your question: am I happy to have chosen the profession of seamstress? Actually, did I ever have a choice of profession? Upon leaving school, I did not exactly see any other possibilities, at least in the short term. The incomes of my mother and my brother are not great, as you know. Therefore I, too, must work to earn my bread (I know you are going to laugh at this expression that is used around me, but not around you!). What is more, daughter and granddaughter of seamstresses, how could I avoid this profession? I live it; I have known its secrets forever! You see, I fall asleep on fabrics; I prick myself on needles fallen on the carpet; I sit down on the needle-booklet, the pincushion. Do not laugh: you did not take your first steps in the bedroom-workshop-living room of a busy seamstress! You know neither the troubles nor the joys of this profession, which both attracts and frustrates me.

So, to go on, I will describe for you (succinctly — do not worry) the two sides of sewing that are at the root of my hesitation, and that will allow me, perhaps, to advance in my "peregrinations" as you say so prettily — even if Sister Theresa would find the word "not really adapted to the context."

On the one hand, on the good hand, there is fashion and, above all, fabrics that fascinate me. Indeed, I have forever adored the touch, the softness, the suppleness, the many textures! It is so easy for me to imagine them on the bodies of women, where they reveal the beauty or hide the imperfections.

There is as much pleasure in deciding on the shape, the assembling, the slightest details! And I am not speaking of the satisfaction we derive when we manage to convince the client that our choices are preferable to hers; that they respond better to her desires, to her needs, to her form. My mother is especially talented in the art of persuasion; she has taught me a lot in this domain, I think.

But let us return to the fabric. You cannot imagine the

excitement mingled with fear that possesses you the moment you go to cut it. Yes, no matter the fabric — silk, wool, serge, batiste, percale, organdy, or others — none of them pardons an error, for it is the earnings of a week or a month that hang on your gesture. Yes, we do not think enough of the hand, the eye, even the back that decide the fate of this warm, light or firm material. Too often we forget the tension that surges at the moment when we must cut, the attention to follow the lines (whether there is a pattern or not). And yet, what pleasure — the scissors at rest — to take hold of these pieces, to unfold them, to admire them, whether the front or the back! Ah! How I love these fabrics, of which most of us ignore both their origin and their production.

In fact, my dear Eugénie, we do not speak often enough of these large bolts, these fabrics of variable thickness; we only see their color and their utility, rarely the miracle of their existence. To understand this miracle, imagine the little sheep in the meadow, the beautiful plant waving in the wind, the little white worm attached to the leaf of the mulberry. And then you must think of the men and women who harvest the wool, linen, hemp, cotton and cocoons of silk worms; you need to salute the spinners, the dyers, the weavers, the winders . . .

You are going to tell me to cut my song short, but it is not so long ago that, with mother and her aunts, we spoke of the textile workers who are so exploited! Men (I think of my uncles and cousins, of course) speak more likely of machines, as these are supposed to solve all the problems of humanity, since they are meant to facilitate the creation of every object that surrounds us. But, concerning fabrics, I see no trace of improvement: its price never goes down, the workers are not paid better, the women work as hard as ever, without respite.

Yes, Eugénie, fabric is all of that! That is why it should be revered, be well treated by the seamstresses, and all of us, the wearers of clothes. But I am digressing, I fly away, as Mother says. And yet, writing all of this to you helps me understand the profession of seamstress and its limits. In effect, to design a dress, choose the material, cut, assemble: all of that pleases me, enthralls me.

However, and this is the bad side of it, one has to actually sew! Sew tight little stitches, really tight, really aligned, really identical! Repeat hour after hour this minuscule gesture; this gesture that tires me, bores me, puts me to sleep. I do not want to live with my fingers grasping needles all day long, my back sore from hours spent on a sewing machine (thank you, Mr. Singer). My fingers, my wrists need gestures that are more generous, more harmonious, more decisive. I need to protect them, to support them, to satisfy them, for they are the key to my success as a musician. Choice or not, seamstress or not, I will not, I cannot interrupt my harp study. And even if I cannot hope some day to earn a decent living playing this subtle instrument, I will stick to it religiously. Sister Theresa would be proud of me, I think.

But I am not going to speak to you of music or my letter would never be finished, and it is not the question that occupies us today. So, my conclusion? I need to find a way to get as close as possible to the fashion world, but not have to sew. How do I do that? I do not know, for the fashion world is rather closed. I am going to ask around. If you have any ideas or contacts, help me rethink all this.

Please, write to me, tell me of your adventures in that land so far away, your progress in that society of do-gooders in our lovely province. I say "our," because a goodly part of Mother's family, the Ansarts, are from Artois.

Many hugs and kisses,
CLO

ℰℐ

PARIS, THURSDAY, AUGUST 20, 1891

My sweet Friend,

Forgive my late response to your letter. Mother sprained her ankle going downstairs; so I am in charge of cooking, shopping, cleaning and, of course, everything related to sewing that requires standing up (taking the client's measurements for instance).

That said, I very much appreciated your letter, for what you told me of your aunt is fascinating. A professional photographer, who owns a studio in her own name, on the Grands Boulevards, in this day and age! That is incredible! How talented she must be, how determined to live from a profession so clearly (up to now) reserved for men! You may tell me that many women work in photographic studios, but most of them are merely employees tucked away in the dark room, or simply retouching. So, to have one's own storefront is a real achievement. This woman is clearly admirable! And her photographs must be truly superb since you say that she has numerous clients. Will she rejoin the great female photographers of whom we speak so rarely — Ernestine Nadar, Angelina Trouillet or Madame Leghait?

I am going to pass by your aunt's studio as soon as possible, to see what she is exhibiting in her window and, perhaps, propose to her my drawing talents in the event she is actually looking for a retouch artist!

You added that, thanks to her talent, she was able to raise alone a son, whose father's name she has kept secret. That leads me to think that your aunt is not afraid to shock the "right-minded" Parisian petite bourgeoisie. That must really scare your parents: they worry that you too will become an artist with a very independent, uncontrollable mind, and thus impossible to marry . . .

That your aunt should choose, today, to wed the love of her youth is more touching than disappointing, as far as I am concerned. Let's wish her much happiness, even if she is somewhat giving up her freedom. But at her age, does freedom have the same meaning as for us? Does it lead to the same decisions? I would not know what to say to that, but your aunt remains no less an admirable person, an example to follow!

My enthusiasm will not surprise you when you know more about my own family. Yes, freedom, the independence of women is a subject of which I have thought for a long time, since there are many women in my circle who have chosen an uncommon and even subversive path! Of course we rarely speak of these divergences out of fear of sullying our family's reputation, but certainly, as far as I am concerned, these women should be the source of our pride!

Here is a little something to surprise you while I explain my position. My mother never knew her father, for he died soon after her birth. Even though he took the time to officially recognize his daughter, he never had the idea, or the time, or the means to marry her mother. A single mother she was and remained. That did not prevent her from raising her daughter very well, nor from living comfortably from her work as a seamstress.

Nonetheless, some questions come to mind. Knowing that we are supposed to protect our virginity up to our wedding night, how did my grandmother (just like your aunt) breach this rule? Was it through weakness or courage, determination or frivolity, passion or independence? Who knows? It is no less true that she must have profoundly loved this man, this Edouard Robin, army quartermaster of fragile health, since she, according to my mother, decided to never marry after his death.

But did she really have a choice? Did she have other crushes, other suitors? Who knows? In addition, would a well-off man have taken up with a single mother, even if her child had been recognized by the father?

All these questions will remain without real answers since my grandmother, this Clotilde whose name I bear, left this world eight days before my birth. But it is no less true that she was able to make of her daughter an energetic person whose strength, in the face of adversity, does not fail to amaze all the members of our family, which is rather extensive, as you know.

I cannot speak to you now of those other women who had, as well, a fate less than ordinary, for "duty calls me" as my brother would say. I will leave you now, but expect some longer letters in a few days, because I must speak to you also of the score of the "Ball," the second movement of the *Symphonie Fantastique* of Berlioz, that I am working on with uncommon joy, given the place reserved for the harp in this piece.

> *Tender hugs and kisses,*
> CLOTILDE

☙❧

TUESDAY, AUGUST 25, 1891

My Eugénie,

Your knowledge in the domain of photography does not cease to astonish me! No, I know nothing of the work of Maria Chambefort, I am sorry to say. But having never traveled to Roanne, and daguerreotypes not being well considered nowadays, you will not be surprised at my ignorance. That being said, I thank you for mentioning this artist who deserves our

13

attention. I will speak of her to my friends for it may be that some of her works are for sale in Paris — and why not in Arras?

Speaking of Arras, where are you in your "friendly" discoveries? Tell me soon about that Sunday dinner. Tell me all about the chamber music concert, and above all of those warm-hearted musicians . . .

Your thoughts about my grandmother are quite right. Indeed, her sentiments for Edouard Robin were, no doubt, shared, since he recognized his daughter, and this, shortly *before* her birth. I must nonetheless add an interesting detail: he, too, was the son of an "unknown" father. Ah yes, may we say that "great minds think alike?" Do not laugh too hard at my impertinence, since that might draw the attention of your mother, and I do not wish to awaken her curiosity about our correspondence . . .

But, coming back to "grandpa" Robin: It may be that his own status as an illegitimate child led him to this act of kindness toward my grandmother. I should add that his mother may have urged him to accept his responsibilities given her own experience. Nonetheless Mother hardly speaks of this woman who died too soon to play a major role in the life of her grandchild beyond some money, and the non-negligible assistance when it came to setting my grandmother up in Paris, on the Île Saint-Louis. In fact, the Robins, being the owners of the building, never asked for rent from the mother of their granddaughter.

What I can tell you of the early death of this "irresistible" soldier, to satisfy your curiosity, is that it was not related to an act of bravery on the battlefield. It seems that an undefined illness took him. Nothing glorious in that case. Too bad!

But getting back to the subject that concerns us: marriage or not. It is clear that the relation between men and women can be remarkably varied. It follows that the women of my family, each of them, had a fate much different from the others; they present us with a panoply of the options available to us. Enough to increase our conception of the role we should play in this society that is ours . . . perhaps.

Take, for instance, my great-grandmother: she was married at 23, to a man her age. Mother of five children, she followed her spouse throughout France, then she ran a tobacco shop up until her widowhood at 78. Her life would seem to illustrate the traditional marriage of the small property owners and shop-keepers.

Her oldest daughter was wedded at age 16, to a 23-year-old optician. She had two sons and worked with her husband who moved from optics to printing, in the west side of Paris. As did her mother, she lived an active life that was based on cooperation with her husband rather than dependence

The second (my grand-mother), an unmarried mother at 18, remained single. She never had to depend on any man other than her father.

The third married at 19, was widowed ten years later, and remarried the same year. Once again widowed, she wed a third man. She had a child by her first husband, a nice fortune from her second, and twenty years of happy life with her third.

The last one, unmarried mother at 18, also, started by the age of 25 to cohabit with a man who gave her three children before marrying her 11 years later. Then he gave her a fourth and final son, and introduced her to the high society of Paris — where she is at home despite the death of her spouse, in 1882, after thirteen years of co-habitation — I think you will appreciate my play on words here.

But, coming back to our subject, four daughters, four very different lives. I might add that the son of this family, having reached his thirties, married a young woman of 20, and gave her two children before she died at age 30; again a traditional marriage, with a sad ending, which is still not rare nowadays, alas!

Do you not find these choices, these fates surprising? Where does the courage of these women, who dared to live beyond the norms, come from? Where did they find the necessary determination to lead lives not very "glorious," yet, in fact, very rich?

Another question must be asked: what sort of union awaits me if it is true that we carry familial traits?

What is also disturbing is our incapacity to foresee and thus to prepare ourselves. We are told to pray to the Lord, and to be optimistic, but are we actually able to choose our own destiny? We are even very far from the simple choice of a husband!

What do you think of all this? Where can we find answers to all our questions? Oh, Eugénie, we have so many uncertainties that it is often hard for me to concentrate my attention on my daily tasks. Fortunately music gives me the necessary lightness and acceptance to reconcile with those around me! I am going to leave you and caress my harp, Edouard having offered to mail this letter which you should receive on Friday.

> *Your friend, who sends you many tender kisses,*
> CLOTILDE

WEDNESDAY, SEPTEMBER 2, 1891

My very dear Friend,

I have been thinking about your questions on the ability of the women in my family to enter society despite their unusual choices. Yes, they knew how to live and accept their fate, and no doubt their amorous passions, that is, if they had any. I doubt that they were acting simply under the pressure of their desire. In fact, they simply showed a great independence of spirit. Little did it matter what people thought of them. They considered their choices as legitimate. All shared the rebellious character of their mother and the very open mind of their father. Thus, they have led lives that are astonishing but also very useful for those around them. And that is the origin of the admiration I feel for them, and about which you wonder. That admiration is due to the fact that they not only played a very important role, even though a very different one, in my life, but they also were remarkable models. I am speaking principally of my mother's two aunts, Emilie and Sara Caroline.

Here are a few details that will enlighten you.

Emilie was eight years younger than my grandmother, and the fourth child. Well-educated, she was, according to Mother, particularly attracted, at a young age, to the arts, especially painting. Perhaps she could have had a career as an artist but, for some unknown reason, she chose to marry, at 19, an army Quartermaster who was in charge of provisioning the troops; most likely a friend of Edouard Robin. She followed him wherever the army took him, in France and in Algeria, for four years; and there is no sign she continued to paint. Had she lost her dream of becoming an artist? Was this man irresist-ible? Not for very long, for she returned to France, supposedly to ensure a good education for her son who was born in 1849. In fact her husband was a real spendthrift and drank heavily. She settled in Paris, also on Saint-Louis Island. Thanks to her brother Candide, she made many friends, above all in the circle of young painters for whom she modeled. When her first husband died in Algeria in 1859, a few months later she remarried one of those artists: Ernest Dellaleau.

When this one died, five years later, she did not remain single — even though he had left her a fortune freeing her from all want. In fact, she quickly married an old friend who was also a painter and art professor at the Sainte-Barbe school, namely our uncle Louis Rouyer, whom you had the pleasure of meeting.

Three husbands in fifteen years, now there is a woman whose fate was very different from that of my grandmother! What is more, she did not have to work a day since her husbands took care of her every need. But did she marry to be free from want, to be simply a spoiled little woman, a model bourgeoise, always in her place? I strongly doubt it! Anyway, my mother often said that it was she who "wore the pants in the family . . ." an interesting expression if ever there was one. In fact, from a little distance, it seems evident to me that she showed independence in her attitude, in her way of doing things and of thinking, rather than simply fulfilling her role as wife.

I think I can go even further: she was in fact a "forceful lady" for, just like her own mother, she played a very important role in all our lives; but a role that went well beyond the help expected from a member of a united family. It was not simply a presence, gifts of money, advice or recommendations. It was quite different. She welcomed us, pampered us, but above all she guided us. She encouraged us to go beyond the norm, beyond what was expected. She pushed us to examine everything under a different light, not to fear the unusual. It is to her, and to uncle Louis, that I owe my love of painting, of music and of reflection of course! It was she who gave me my first harp when I was only 10. It was she who encouraged Edouard to pursue cabinetry. It was she who pushed cousin Alexander toward engraving rather than becoming a bureaucrat.

No, she was not the provincial bourgeoise that some wanted

to see in her. She was a remarkable, extremely generous woman who inspired us all. She never profited from others, she dedicated her life to them.

I will leave you here, my Dear, for I am too moved to pursue this letter. Meanwhile, my silence will no doubt hone your curiosity . . .

⌘

My Eugénie,

I take up my letter again, because it is time to speak of the fate of Caroline, my mother's youngest aunt; another fate that was not ordinary, as you could see in my last letter.

This last born of the family had a brief relationship with a young Parisian who, carried away by revolutionary ideas, died on the barricades in 1848. He left Caroline pregnant and with no spouse, when she was only 18. The family welcomed the child with real tenderness, which truly comforted the young mother.

Confident and determined, she did not lose hope of finding another man; which came to pass six years later. I should add that she was quite intelligent, pretty, impish, and full of a charm that a captain of dragoons could not resist. She followed him to Algeria where she gave birth to their first son. Upon returning to France, she had two other boys with this lover who had not obtained (or perhaps not sought) the permission of the military hierarchy to marry her. For her it was no obstacle to her happiness. Of independent mind, she never tried to get him to marry her. She asked for nothing other than to live near the one she loved. What others thought was of no consequence to her. On the other hand, she was truly spoiled by this man who was fifteen years older. When he left the army, he wished to marry her and recognize his three sons. She acquiesced, and a fourth son was born a year later.

Admit, this fate is not ordinary, insofar as this captain was, in fact, a lover of literature, and a member of the Parisian gentry . . . You see now of whom I am speaking.

But how can we explain this decision to "live in sin," to live so far from the norms of her day? And that without a moment's hesitation! It must be said that she was, always, solidly aided by her family — the second and third boys were born at their grandparents' home in la Ferté-Gaucher, and carried their name until their father recognized them. It happened that neither Sarah nor her parents considered "legitimacy" to be a barrier to happiness.

After reflecting a little and an interesting discussion with Mother, I think I can say that their freedom of action is certainly related to their admiration for the idealists of this century and their disciples.

Yes, my friend, the Guyots (especially the men) were, and still are, admirers of the idealistic philosophy of Saint-Simon. Do not laugh: many members of French industry followed this humanist's thinking. And still today, there are many of these groups actively committed. They rally around the ideas of Prosper Enfantin, a graduate of the École Polytechnique, as you know, who greatly advanced the world of science. For the women of my family, it is above all the vision of Charles Fourier that is appealing. In effect, they have espoused the vision of an ideal world where women share the sexual freedom of men, where illegitimate children are legitimate, where the wages of everyone are calculated on the quality of the work and not on the gender or personality of the worker.

We are far from having achieved that ideal today, as you

know, but if you read carefully *L'Intransigeant* or *Le Parti Ouvrier* newspapers, you will see that the future and well-being of all workers are at the heart of the discussions dealing with French industry. And the labor unions are multiplying in rhythm with the strikes much to the annoyance of the industrialists . . .

Well, I stepped away from our main topic that is so close to our heart: women's freedom and their vision of marriage. I am coming back to it because the union of Aunt Caroline touches on another concept, that of belonging to the nobility . . . Oh yes, we can be *fouriériste*[1] and still remain attached to the royalist segment of our society: as the fate of our revolutions shows well enough — it could happen that the Count of Orléans succeeds President Sadi Carnot who is so attached to the Republic . . . Do not laugh, but this could explain why Caroline and her parents wanted to put the family back into the ranks of the petite noblesse, no matter their ideology! After all, you must know that grandmother Guyot was an Ansart de Bofle et de Marcon; a member of the gentry of the Artois whose descendants you have met. And that handsome captain of dragoons was none other than a Count. There! A perfect opportunity to restore the faded crest of the Ansarts! It could also be that the Count had chosen Caroline because she belonged, as did he, to the nobility of the gown:[2] the count's ancestors were parliamentarians while the Ansart were bailiffs.

Furthermore, according to my brother, the count's brother had only daughters — four of them in all. But the number and the legitimacy of daughters do not make them successors to the title, as we know! So the sons of Caroline insured that the title of Count would not disappear. You will admit that this small detail bears mentioning, above all if it is the key to the late marriage, completely legal, of Caroline and the Count.

However, we should not judge the choices of my great aunt on these assumptions (of somewhat pernicious character) for we must recognize that her charm is not based on her status as Countess, but on her personality. And her influence on the members of our family is much deeper than we can believe. For us she is elegance, beauty, and savoir-faire incarnate, and benevolence as well. She is at ease in any situation, she always finds the right words, the words that reassure or soothe. She knows how to use her contacts to help those who need it. And she has, what is more, a generous wit — which makes her table and her parlor places sought after with enthusiasm. Her generosity is well known: her servants adore her, her gardener kneels before her, the children fight to touch her hand or her dress, and dogs follow at her heel. She is literally The Lady. She would find my list rather excessive, for this great lady knows also how to show humility, which is rarely the case in this posh company.

I know that you will look at her with more attention, now that you are aware of her qualities — in every sense of the word.

There you have my Friend, a more complete but right description of these women who have marked us so. Thanks to them, we have a more open or rather richer vision of life; we know now that our options are not limited to "traditional" marriage. We can, like them, feel freer and more engaged in our activities and talents; we may live our dreams . . .

On these words full of hope, I send you kisses and say "until soon."

Your faithful friend,
CLO

❧

TUESDAY, SEPTEMBER 15, 1891

My sweet Eugénie,

I really enjoyed your letter, which arrived this morning. Ah yes, writing, above all to those I love and who share my tastes, is a real pleasure for me. But I am not certain to be, as you suggest, the Madame de Sévigné of our times! First of all the subjects I raise are very personal and intended only for those to whom I write — you in particular. What is more, who would dare to compare herself to that writer? But, humble as I am, I must say that your humor gave me much pleasure.

I should add that, according to my uncle Louis, the letters that we read in class, which inspired us all, had been extensively edited, at the time of their publication, since the granddaughter of Madame de Sévigné found them to be rather "non-conforming to the norms of decorum." I have a hard time imagining what those letters could have revealed to be thus modified. What is certain is that, illustrious or not, no one is safe from the arrogance of their relatives. I hope that no one in my family or yours would dare to edit my letters before you have a chance to read them!

You might be surprised at the ease with which we share our secrets. But for me the basis of friendship is that we have no "secrets" from each other. This sharing permits us to think with insight and also, I believe, to better understand who we are. By "opening our windows," fresh air enters us, we are better able to breathe, see and understand others in their reality. This is what the necessity, the beauty of sharing is. What worth have our thoughts without those of others?

I would add briefly that our society wants us to be discreet — yes, we have to show discretion, all the time; but this only reinforces the lies! What is more, if we ignore what affects the lives of others, we will commit errors of judgment, we will be less likely to trust them; we will be unable to live in harmony. It

23

is the fear of others' judgments that forces us to remain silent. But this is detrimental to all relations, be they professional, familial or amorous, or even simply neighborly. Indeed, how can we hope to help each other if we do not know each other's concerns, or what governs one's choices? And that is true in every important domain!

You see, my Eugénie, we are right to share our family secrets, for they explain many things. I will give you another example that cannot fail to astonish you and, perhaps, disturb you, so forgive my frankness.

I have known for a long time that your father is a Freemason. No, you did not tell me; do not worry! I heard it from my brother, who is also one, just like my grandfather, cousins and uncles. They are members of the same Lodge. That is comforting for you, right? But here is my first question: why are these men from our family so eager to hide their vows, given that Masonry played such an important role in both their careers and their choice of a spouse; and, of course, in their social status, as well as their attitude towards society? My brother told me that the Freemasons came up, way before the 1789 revolution, with the motto of our Republic: "Liberté Egalité Fraternité!!"

Yes, they definitely are progressive, empathetic men who always help their fellow men. Why hide all that? Is it because the Church has been opposed to any form of organization that might put it in the shadows? Without a doubt. But today, since our society is keeping its distance from the episcopal hierarchy, why hide any affiliation so carefully? I would add that the beliefs of both sides follow the same morality: assistance, respect for others, compassion — if I have understood what was instilled in us in our little school, and every Sunday at mass!

There you are, my dear one, I have shared my thoughts with

you on this "taboo" subject. What will you be teaching me in your next letter?

Tender hugs and kisses from your Clo

WEDNESDAY, SEPTEMBER 23, 1891

My dearest Friend,

Your letter really made me laugh. So, my Eugénie is not convinced by the young men of Arras, despite their many attempts! I am trying to imagine them demanding the next dance, congratulating you on your grace and your Parisian elegance. Nonetheless perhaps one of them deserves your attention, above all if he is a tenor or a baritone. Think of this possibility. That said, I also have a story to share that should interest you.

My cousin Paul assured me at dinner yesterday evening, that he would not hesitate to fight a duel to save my honor. Military mentality, if ever there was!

I know that a young captain belonging to the lesser Parisian nobility has preserved the privilege of fighting duels, but really, I was more dumbfounded than honored if I may say so. I did not know what to say to him, nor could I thank him for his gallantry, as the conversation, thank God, took another direction.

But there is something there to think about. Defend our honor! Why would we need a man to defend our honor? And why with weapons? How could killing or wounding someone possibly restore this supposedly lost honor? Now that is an absurd notion, above all if one does not know how to better define our "honor!"

Do you follow me in this labyrinth, in these thoughts that are just a little nebulous? Honor, in fact, is the respect shown to us by others. But this respect is not simply based on our ability to keep men at a distance, at least I hope not! It is actually the result of our attitude, our tendency to show compassion and esteem to others. I feel completely capable of doing that, and thus to take myself in hand. Honestly! So, no thank you, my dear Captain!

As for music, I am not sure I told you that I shall take part in a little concert at the end of October, at the Mesureurs'. Their daughter being a very talented violinist, they asked me to join with her to entertain their guests. We will be playing two pieces that emphasize the harp, and benefit from the melodic richness of the violin. You know these two pieces very well: "Un Bal" from Berlioz's *Symphonie Fantastique,* since it contains a harp solo, and Beethoven's "La Bagatelle" in A minor, better known as "Für Elise." Do not take offense at the lack of a piano; our duo with harp and violin will be a novelty that should satisfy our audience. So now you understand why I am so excited!

There, my Eugénie, tell me as soon as possible what you think of all this, before getting involved with brio in the meanderings of this dancing and well-meaning society of Arras. And, above all, give me more details about the voice teacher to whom you were recommended, and that you will meet Friday. I know that you will amaze him, and that you will be preparing for some concerts very soon to impress your new friends and acquaintances.

With many hugs and kisses,
CLOTILDE

My dear, dear Eugénie,

Just a quick word to thank you for your good wishes. Yes, being 19 is a privilege: people are beginning to listen to me a little whenever I dare make a suggestion (not give advice), and I can choose the dress I will wear tomorrow without a comment from Mother, or from my brother! I am joking, a little, of course, but you know what I am talking about — we will remain little girls, until some man marries us, I suppose. But I cannot complain since I received a great many lovely cards (like yours) and a little vial of Roger et Gallet eau de cologne: so I am all ready to meet Queen Victoria, who was seduced by these perfumers, according to Aunt Caroline!

I want to share another bit of good news with you: last Sunday I went to visit the Renaults, in Boulogne-Billancourt with Aunt Caroline, Jules and Paul. They were neighbors of my aunt when she lived in Boulogne, and you met them once or twice when they were visiting her Rue du Ranelagh. It seems Aunt Caroline is often in touch with them, undoubtedly because they are very charming, very open, and extremely helpful.

So Sunday the atmosphere was particularly joyful because their youngest son, Louis, who is almost 14, had installed electricity in their "weekend retreat" (as Berthe Renault would say as a true tourangelle). This boy is shy and reserved, but he will go far, according to his father and even his brothers, who mock him a bit because of his passion for mechanics. Personally I find Fernand, who is 25, nicer, but Marcel is the funniest. Five months my senior, he seems much older than me, according to my brother, who is a little jealous of him, I think. I might mention that their father has passed the management of his sewing materials business to his two elder sons; perhaps because his health is not what it used to be, although no one mentioned it.

But let us get to the good news: during the meal our hosts asked me several questions about my work and activities. This led me to express my uncertainty about dressmaking. Monsieur Renault proposed to introduce me to the representative of the Furnion Company, one of his fabric suppliers. These manufacturers started to use the painting-on-silk technique two years ago. This is a very complicated technique, which interests me greatly. It would be fascinating to work in this area! Thus you understand then, my Eugénie, how impatient I am to meet this man, which should happen this month. Let us hope! So the day in Boulogne was not only enjoyable, but also very useful. Another reason to admire the interpersonal skills of Aunt Caroline.

Before closing, I must say that I admire your determination: it will take you far! In addition, your reasoning is very convincing; certainly by joining the choir of the Cathedral of Arras, you will have numerous occasions to sing solos, and of course to display your immense talent. Believe me, in a short while they will be flocking to your appearances in the most sought after concert halls of Artois, Flanders, and Picardie! I must now get to work on my harp, since the 19TH of October is not far off, but I continue to think of you and your projects.

Your Clotilde with much love

❦

My dear Eugénie,

Your letter, which arrived Wednesday as you thought, brought me great pleasure; thank you for your wishes. I am indeed busy with my rehearsals at the Mesureurs'. Suzanne and I get along really well and I think we will be ready to greet our public on Sunday the 26. I must add that the Erard harp that they borrowed is of exceptional quality. How lucky I am! It is a pity that you will not be able to be with us on that day! But I promise to play the pieces for you and your family, when you come to Paris in December — even if my little harp is not comparable.

Another subject: Mother and I are going to see your grandmother next week to adjust and repair her black winter coat. It will be an excellent opportunity to talk about you, and to admire your beautiful portrait on the living room mantel. Your grandmother is so lucky to have a granddaughter who is so pretty and talented, and you to have a grandmother so devoted and generous! I am always indebted to her for having introduced me to Madame Huisman, to whom I owe my passion for music, and above all for the harp. If she had not left us so soon, I would be part of the orchestra at the Opera. I am joking, of course, but it is no less true that her teaching is the basis of all my knowledge, of all my abilities as a harpist.

As far as I am concerned, I see the friendship that united these two great ladies as the key to my fate as a musician. Do not tell me I am a little crazy, for if God has worked in this manner, they too have played an essential role. I hope that our friendship will bring, in a half century, a similar happiness to some girl as lucky as I am!

Mother is asking for my help, so I will stop here, but I promise to tell you as soon as possible what happens this coming Sunday.

A thousand hugs,
CLOTILDE

ᥱᥬ

My sweet Friend

I must tell you right away that everything went well yesterday at the Quai de Gesvres,[3] in the beautiful salon overlooking the Seine. Yes, thirty attentive people so very impressed by our little concert that every one stood and applauded us! I must say that Suzanne, for all of her eight years, is truly prodigious. I do not know if I told you that she has been playing the violin for the last four years — I was already seven before I was allowed to tap on the keys of the piano that my grandfather was building.

In short, we got a standing ovation (as they say, so well, in the language of Shakespeare) and hugs, handshakes and many excellent little cookies. Our Congressman and his lady showed themselves to be very gracious and grateful to me. Aunt Caroline assured me that I had made some friends upon whom I could "count." That is not what interests me today, because what "counts" for me, is to touch the listener, it's to always feel that indescribable joy of performing.

So, my Eugénie, you understand by my enthusiasm, that even if I deplore your absence, I am in excellent spirits because there is more than this success at the salon. Indeed, during the tea that followed our concert, Mr. de Berlantier, a good friend of the Mesureurs, came up to me: my playing apparently made a big impression on him. I am still completely surprised, but above all delighted! He asked me a few questions. The most interesting "and why the harp?" surprised me, above all since I did not want to give him a long exposé of my life. So I was hesitating when this phrase came to me: "We do not choose an instrument, it chooses us!" Apparently my answer pleased him for he complimented me again on my talent. When he learned that I did not often have the opportunity to play before a large group, he proposed to recommend me to the Concert Master at the Madeleine Church. It seems the regular harpist is in poor health (the misfortune of one makes the fortune of others, as Mother often says). You can imagine my stupor: to play under the baton of Gabriel Fauré, who could ask for more? And that without a diploma from the Conservatory!

I am going to the Madeleine tomorrow to get a sense of the place and the harp. Thus I will not seem to be too pitiful if I have the honor to be presented to this great man, Sunday, after the high mass. In addition, I am working with dedication on the "Prelude in C Major" of Johann Sebastian Bach, which I will play if this meeting comes to pass. I tremble at the idea. My friend, pray, pray for me!

To satisfy your curiosity, or rather your customary sagacity, I must admit that the laughing eyes of my "benefactor" are full of charm, and they regarded me with more attention than I would like, but his generosity and his perfect tact lead me to accept this state of affairs. I plan to keep my distance and behave like the young girl full of modesty and respect that every patron should expect from his "protégé," no more, no less. I will write to you soon to let you know if this artistic meeting has taken place, but do not leave me without news!

> *Yours,*
> CLO

ↄ⌀

WEDNESDAY, NOVEMBER 4, 1891

My dear One,

Your letter, which came this morning, filled me with joy: you will be here, in front of me, in nine days, what a thrill!

I will not offer to go meet you at the train, since you will not arrive in Paris until 8 o'clock in the evening, and only if the train is not late — as Edouard mentioned when I asked him if he could accompany me. He also pointed out how far the Gare Saint-Lazare is from our Faubourg Saint-Antoine, especially when you cannot afford to take a carriage. But I will be free all of Sunday and will let your grandmother know. It is up to you to decide on a suitable time for my visit rue de Reuilly.

It is useless to say how much I wish your visit were longer. Three days in Paris is very short, but I will be happy with whatever time you can give me. Above all since I have another wonderful piece of news to share: the choirmaster, Mr. Fauré, has agreed to meet with me on the 20TH of November. Yes, you can imagine how excited I am.

I am working on my music every day for hours, to the chagrin of my mother who is very busy lately. I do my best to help her, but it is necessary to favor my music, right?

I have never been so excited in all my life!

Thank you, thank you, my Friend for listening to me with so much patience!

> *Many hugs and kisses,*
> YOUR CLOTILDE

℘

MONDAY, NOVEMBER 25, 1891

My sweet Friend,

I do not need to tell you how much I appreciate these moments we spend together: you are the only person in whom I can confide. What luck to have you for a friend! And what pleasure to know that you share the same feelings! Your mother is right to say that December 20 will arrive quickly, but my impatience is not abating . . .

But let us get to the "news" as I promised to tell you everything about the meeting with our great Fauré. Well, I will simply say that my anxiety was misplaced, as you will see.

I entered the church and the sacristan led me into the little room where our great Choir Master was speaking with the parish priest. He was facing the open door, and smiled upon seeing us enter. The priest turned around wondering no doubt what could be making Fauré smile. The latter came toward me and said, tilting his head: "Mademoiselle Loeven, I suppose." I must have blushed while performing the little curtsy expected of a young lady. He then introduced me to the priest saying that I had come to show him my talents as harpist. I blushed even harder while trying to show him my loveliest smile, though without showing my teeth: propriety obviously being in order.

I had never seen him up close, so I was charmed by his smiling eyes. With a large forehead, a nice mustache and a discrete little goatee, he is rather handsome. Also, he stands very straight but his attitude is not at all condescending. No do not worry, he is a little too old for us, and he is married, I think.

He invited me to go into the room where the harp is stored. He asked me all sorts of questions about my training, which works I prefer, then he asked me to play "Un Bal" by Berlioz — as luck would have it, unless Monsieur de Berlantier mentioned the success of our little October concert to his friend . . .

After that, I played a little Bach. He was watching me with close attention tilting his head here and there. I must have done well, for he stopped me and said: "Very good Mademoiselle, come on Thursday for choir rehearsal and we will speak about our agreement."

He then excused himself for leaving so suddenly; one of his students was waiting for him in Neuilly. Upon leaving the Madeleine, he hailed a carriage, which left at a trot. I made my way to the rue de Rivoli to take the tram. I waited more than twenty minutes, but I was so overexcited (thank you Monsieur Pothey for this very explicit word!) that I lost track of time. It was only upon arriving home when mother asked me why I was so late, that I understood how the time had escaped me.

Yes, my friend, I am still completely stunned; I did not expect the ease with which I was able to convince the great Fauré. How lucky I am, how happy! I pray that you find a similar happiness when you are hired to sing at the Arras Opera in the near future.

I will leave you, for it is very late and I have to get up early tomorrow morning.

Your friend who loves you dearly,
CLOTILDE

෫෭

THURSDAY, FEBRUARY 9, 1892

My so dear Friend,

I am happy that my card arrived just in time for your Saint's Day my "almost saint" Eugénie, and that you liked the design and the colors. I bought it, as you may imagine, at our little paper store on the Boulevard Diderot. The store owner's son recognized me as soon as I entered as he quickly asked me how my friend was. Apparently he has not forgotten your charm nor your delicate taste for beautiful postcards! I can see your smile all the way from here . . .

Memories, memories, but today, how I would like to be near you to meet all those people who will become your friends! But beware: the handsome Emile may make promises to you that he cannot keep. And he is two years younger than you are, something that is not done in our milieu. Men must be older than we are and too bad if they are nearly senile . . .

As for my cousins d'Argis, you have very little chance: Henri, as you may know, does not care for women (to the great disappointment of his family), even though he hides his preference with great skill — except in his books, which, by the way, are not easy to find. Do not expect anything from Alphonse or Paul, for your father is only "an honorable and honored administrator" not a large property owner. Indeed, for these members of the French gentry, property is the only sure thing (and, what is more, indispensable) at least for the last generation or two. Thus, my dear friend, seek out other sentimental horizons: look for the love bird without thinking too much of tomorrow, while "keeping your distance . . ." If that does not work, do not fret, you know your parents will find you someone worthy (in their eyes); a colonial governor for instance, to satisfy your taste for travel. And the opera in all of that?

On my end, some good news: the rehearsals at the Madeleine Church are going well. Everyone welcomed me nicely and seems to appreciate my modest talent. Also, the harpist for whom I substitute may not come back as soon as planned. An additional year would be ideal!

Moreover, my work for the Blanchet company, the fabric wholesalers, is interesting. Indeed, we have to determine what our ladies will want to wear this spring: fabrics with colors rather dark, yet very nuanced. Silk and percale are also more colorful. My role is so far limited, but I am learning a lot about the weaving and dying of the fabrics. That leaves me enough time in the evenings to work on my harp and my drawings.

By the way, I have not received an offer from Furnion & Co, but I am not discouraged. The drawings I sent to Lyon might, finally, convince the administrator in charge of recruiting to include me among his artists. I hope to have more to tell you next week.

Hoping to read you soon, my friend.

With all my love,

CLO

PARIS, WEDNESDAY MARCH 2, 1892

My very dear Eugénie,

Just a quick word, to tell you that we are moving this week, as I mentioned last month.

Here is our new address: 27, rue de la Forge Royale. Yes, right next to the Passage Saint-Bernard, but with a little extra room where Mother will put her sewing machine and her fabrics. This will free up, a little, a large dining room/work room/studio — but not for wood-carving; Edouard is keeping the little workshop in the Passage that he shares with our cousin, Alexandre Guyot. Staying so close allows us to not have to change our routines, as Mother points out.

Otherwise nothing very important to tell you about our Parisian life — except that I just reread with great pleasure the short story by Henry Gréville, *Le Fil d'Or*, that appeared in *Le Figaro Illustré* in April, last year. I found it by chance while emptying out a drawer. What talent this lady has! She knows how to touch her readers. I am waiting impatiently to read *Le Moulin à Vent* that just appeared this week in *Le Figaro* and that my cousin Jules promised to lend me.

You remember how much we loved *L'Avenir d'Aline* and *Chant de Noces*, and how excited we were when my cousin Jules, who is well known in the publishing world, told us that the writer's real name what in fact Alice Durand? I cannot fathom how a writer so popular and prolific had to choose a man's name to be able to publish her books! Yes, a man's name to find her place in the literary world — as did George Sand, by the way. And Daniel Stern, Daniel Lesueur, Charles de Launey, or also André Léo . . . When will our Women of Letters be able to make a name without having to hide behind a masculine pen name? In a century or two? The thought is appalling. So I will go on to a more pleasant subject: You.

Yes, you and your life in Artois. Indeed, I must say that the attentions of this Monsieur Pierre toward you (attentions that you named so precisely in your letter!) seem quite touching and should reassure you: this gentleman is undoubtedly a kindhearted man. Send me more details about him that your parents seem to appreciate, so that I can picture him better — while waiting to receive his photo, if he ever had one taken (you are the only one with whom I can make this sort of pleasantry!). Nonetheless I imagine him as handsome as he is nice. Am I right? Should I infer that you have totally forgotten your little guy we met in Blois? Not a bad thing . . .

This letter was supposed to be short, but as always I have too many things to tell you. Oh, my Eugénie, I am so eager to be near you to share these moments that are so important in our lives! But I must return to my packing; there is still so much to do to empty the rooms that we have occupied for more than eight years!

I will write to you as soon as we are nicely settled in to our new place.

> *Many kisses from your friend,*
> Clo

༺༻

My very dear Friend, (Alfred de Berlantier)

I hope that your trip brought you the exhilaration you wanted, and that the beauty of Italy compensates for the absence of your dearest friends — of whom I hope to be one.

On my end, little to tell you, other than we are very happy in the rue de la Forge Royale. You were right, the move was a very good one, and your assistance in all that was much appreciated. Our dear mother asks me to send you her love and gratitude.

I am so happy to finally have a corner to myself, while waiting to have my own room where I will be able to work on my harp, and draw or write without disturbing anyone. But Edouard maintains that I am becoming so demanding that no man will want me . . . Is the opposite true? Will my charming brother find a woman willing to take him as he is, if one considers that he had his own room upon our settling in at 82 rue Saint-Bernard, even though he was barely 16? We must admit, by way of excuse, that it was his studio as well, and that we found shavings and sawdust even in his bed! Part of the charm of sculpting, no doubt! Now he can work late in his workshop and climb up to his little room without awakening us.

Mother appreciates not having to share the dining room table with me when she is working on her dressmaking. As for me, the little drop leaf table (signed Jean-Louis Loeven) that you found so pretty, and the lovely folding screen, which you gave me, are sufficient.

I must now leave you to deliver a few garments to clients. I will also mail this on the way.

Pray to Saint Mary, excuse me, to Santa Maria when you admire the frescoes of Filippo Lippi, in her church!

> *Your friend,*
> CLO

P.S.: I suppose you are in Florence, but if you are already in Rome, I hope the concierge will forward my letter to you.

WEDNESDAY, MARCH 30, 1892

My dear You, *(Alfred de Berlantier)*

You have been so quiet these last two weeks; did you not receive my letter of the 17TH? Or perhaps you are so overcome by those Italian beauties (of the artistic kind, I mean . . .)?

However, I am not writing to chide, but to share with you some GREAT news. News that has altered the life of my cousins d'Argis. Have you guessed? Alphonse is engaged! Yes, the marriage will take place in mid-October. Unexpected? Of course, but the young woman is really pretty and from a quite respectable family! Perhaps Alphonse had already told you of his desire to marry, but he had said nothing to me about it. I might add, that from his lofty 35 years, he considers me to be more or less a child. Nonetheless, his future bride will be a mere 22 at the beginning of April. I am thrilled at the thought of having a cousin my own age.

The chosen girl's father is a businessman who owns several properties, one of which just happens to be on Ranelagh Street. So, as you can tell, Jeanne is a very good match. She is also very sweet, and timid enough to accept our Alphonse's rather bold character. I am thrilled for them!

And thus the first of four brothers is more or less married off. Aunt Caroline is happy to see Alphonse in a position that assures the continuation of her dear departed husband's name. Let us hope that Paul, my twin, so to speak, who is already a non-commissioned officer with the Dragoons, will have a brilliant military career and earn, as did his father before him, the Legion of Honor! Then he, too, might find a wealthy Jeanne who is eager to marry him.

After this good start, I doubt not that Jules, who will

celebrate his thirtieth just in time for his brother's wedding, will follow the brilliant example set by his elder. Who could resist his charm? What is more, I imagine him choosing a wife older than himself since he loves to take forbidden paths, especially if the chosen one is so rich that her fortune "makes her worth the candle" (I love that old-fashioned expression, especially when the bets are on).

As for Henri, things are a bit more complicated. Was it not you who told me that, in spite of his brilliant success in medical school, the more posh Paris clinics will not hire him because of the scandal that arose from his last two novels? I confess to not having read them: sodomy is a forbidden subject in our milieu, even though Fourier and Proudhon have tried to make the practice accepted, as you undoubtedly know.

I have some tasks to complete for tomorrow, so I leave you to your worthy or less-worthy projects. Still, I hope to have been the first one to tell you this remarkable news! What do you have to say about it, you who are so proud to have avoided, up till now, the pitfalls of marriage?

> *I send hugs, but remember that I eagerly await*
> *word from you!*
> CLOTILDE

TUESDAY, JUNE 7, 1892

My dearest Eugénie,

Your card arrived just in time: last night it was the crown atop five others on my little table, while our family was gathered together to celebrate Saint Clotilde and spoil me! But before I describe our wonderful evening, I want to say how much I love your letters and cards, and of course your good wishes!

Since you insist on having some details of my saint's day, I will say that it began early because, at 9:00, Edouard brought me a beautiful bouquet of anemones intermixed with some flowering branches of mock orange that he had bought at the florist on Aligre Square. In just a few minutes, the bouquet's delicious fragrance filled the whole apartment, and the living room was transformed! Even Mother smiled with pleasure.

Toward noon, the concierge came upstairs to give me my letters, which in fact had come yesterday or the day before, but Mother had undoubtedly orchestrated this postponement of the mail "until the right time . . ." Then, at the end of the day, Aunt Caroline and my cousins, Jules and Paul, arrived with a beautiful cake that we enjoyed with a very sweet muscat that Jules gets from his little grocery at the corner of Carmes Street, the one where we found that blackberry jam that was so delicious we finished the whole jar the same day, do you remember?

Conversation was lively and funny. In fact, lifting his glass to toast me, my cousin Jules offered to take me to the basilica of Sainte Clotilde for Sunday morning mass. According to him, that would be the best way to celebrate my saint's day! That certainly goes to show his sense of humor, since he deigns step into a church only for weddings and funerals! But Mama, the good Catholic that she is, found the idea quite tempting. I have to say that the basilica is beautiful and is well worth a visit when there is a mass, especially during Pentecost. I told Jules that I would certainly take him at his word, if it were not for the distance. In fact, Las Cases Street is much more than just a couple steps away from our Faubourg. Paul pointed out that we would have fewer difficulties finding a bus seat on Sunday. Jules, as a nobleman, proposed that we hire a carriage, his treat. How generous of him! Another nice day to come for your Clotilde's future!

In conclusion, I must admit to being spoiled by all those whom I love, and all thanks to the good saint for whom I was named. But I have not yet met a Clovis to marry, and then to convert. Maybe next time.

And you, have you seen that Mr. Pierre with irresistible charms again? Tell me soon!

Have a great Sunday, even though it is not your saint's day yet!

Many hugs and kisses.

YOUR CLO

∽

Dear Uncle Louis,

How can I ever thank you for your generosity? You have so many nephews and grandnephews in your family, and yet you have thought of me and pampered me more than I deserve! The photography session was a total surprise! I am including in my letter the portrait that your friend made of me in his superb studio. You must admit that it is a very pretty photo. I appear to be so demure, but "do not be fooled by appearances," says Edouard, who has been teasing me without mercy for the last two days. Thank you then, thank you a thousand times for this beautiful birthday present, and for being so present in our lives, despite the distance.

You did not mention your health, nor what occupies your life now that you have given up your mayoral sash. Lumbres and its city hall must bemoan your absence, for you did so much for your constituents and your village. But you, do you miss your office and your duties? Are you thinking of writing a few more books on pedagogy?

Of course Mother and I are praying that life brings you yet more sweet moments, and that your nurse looks after you as well as possible. We hope, too, that you get to spend some long evenings with your friends the Deherlys. They are so charming! Of course, you must miss Aunt Emily very much. You are, both of you, always in our thoughts.

Before closing, I must tell you that the last paragraph of your letter made me wonder: is it such a major event to be 20 years old? Is it such a precious moment? You who have so much experience of things and beings, do you think that yesterday was one of the best days of my life? I hope not, for, truth to tell, I feel rather sad. You see, my birthday follows by a few days the anniversary of the death of my grandmother Clotilde — you probably remember that she passed away a week before my birth — an anniversary that always saddens Mother, at least that is what she says. I think rather that my father's departure, ten years ago now, is the real cause of this melancholy that I also share: none of us has gotten over his desertion . . . Oh! How cruel men can be sometimes!

But I should follow your example and be a little more optimistic, more aware of the good deeds of everyone towards me, more thankful. I have the good luck to be loved, to be spoiled like a little girl. And then, there are all the wonders of this world: music, paintings . . . so you are right, it is great to be 20!

> *With all my love and gratitude,*
> Your Clotilde

P.S.: I am taking the liberty to enclose a photo of Edouard taken last March, the day before his 26TH birthday. Thanks to his tiny moustache, my "big" brother looks more and more like a Loeven! Am I right?

❦

*Edouard
Loeven at
26.*

Clotilde in 1902, a photograph taken to celebrate her 30th birthday

Chapter II
An Unexpected Love Life

Letters from January 1893 to January 1905 sent to

Eugénie

Auguste Guyot, her cousin

Alfred de Berlantier, her friend and mentor

Alexandre and Rose Guyot, parents of Auguste

Jean-Louis Leroy, her lover

My dear, dear Friend, (Alfred de Berlantier)

Forgive me for getting directly into the heart of the matter, but I cannot wait any longer to share my excitement with you: I just spent the most amazing afternoon of my life; I am swept away by this beauty, this unimaginable, surpassing beauty! Let me say, first of all, that my excitement has but one name: Gabriel Fauré.

But before proceeding, I want so much to thank you, for if I have been playing with the Madeleine choir, for the last thirteen months, it is thanks to you!

As for this amazing news: you must know that yesterday, our Choir master asked the members of the choir and instrumentalists to gather today by 1pm without fail. When he saw that all of his people were gathered around him in the Eastern chapel, he announced that his "little" requiem was revised, a bit developed, and virtually completed. He had worked furiously on it, and we had to start digging into our scores right away, as he wanted to present his masterpiece on the 21ST, that is to say two weeks from now! Can you imagine our bewilderment? Our panic? Really? He must have read all that on our faces because, without adding another word, he sat at the little organ, which stands behind the choir, and played the fourth movement: "Pie Jesu" which is most likely to seduce us, to convince us. Within a minute my soul took flight! I simply lost all sense of time. And yet, this piece lasts but a few minutes. When the organ stopped, we were all entranced, incredulous: how had he managed to so enchant us — literally — by playing on this rather mediocre instrument? You see, this is Fauré's genius. He always takes us right to the limits of comprehension.

Some of the musicians and choir singers had a knowing look and were smiling at one another: they had been part of the great event five years ago: that is at the concert on January 16, 1888. As you might remember, Fauré presented the first version of "The Little Requiem" for the funeral of Mr. Le Soufaché, quite prominent an architect at the time. We were at this particular event with the d'Argis, and I remember that Aunt Caroline expressed her surprise at the limited presence of violins in the orchestra. I was enthralled by this requiem, and did not miss the violin, focused as I was on the work of the harpist!

My God, I was barely older than most of our choirboys today! By the way, I heard this afternoon, that Louis Aubert, who now wears sideburns — if not a beard, was only ten or eleven years old and the soloist (he still had his soprano voice). You know that trebles are still preferred to women sopranos, at the Madeleine . . . when will we hear a woman's voice in this august place? But I should not complain given that my way of playing the harp is apparently appreciated!

But let us come back to the new Requiem, which according to Fauré lasts only thirty-five minutes, that is about five minutes per movement. Yes, I do simplify a bit, but, what is more important, is the decision of our Master to give the stage to the low voice strings rather than to the violin; there is only one among the eighteen instruments in this orchestra. This way Fauré underlines the soberness of the moment, and brings forward the voice of the sopranos and the altos that are supported by the violas, the cellos and the contrabass. Of course much room is given to the organ to sustain the choir, but it is the harp which best frames the voice of the young soloist, in the fourth and, above all, in the seventh movement, the "Paradisium." Yes, it is truly a little bit of Heaven that enters into your soul when listening to this movement! An amazing musical feast, which leads you directly to God!

Ah, my dear friend, how the pure voices of our young singers are brought to the fore! You too will be enraptured, you, the circumspect, you the rational, you the guarded one!

And, the harp plays its part, too! So, if you listen attentively and do not get too distracted by the flutes or the cellos, you will hear my accompaniment. It will be as soft and yet as firm as I can make it, for I must be heard, I must hold my place in the interstices, I must contribute without fail to this harmony all along. That this "Pie Jesu" is a deeply moving aria no longer needs to be proven; and that the "Paradisium" and the "Libera me" are truly uncommon in requiems written until now: this is the surprising beauty of this work. But it is also the root cause of the anguish that torments me: will we be able to give this magnificent requiem what it deserves?

My dear, dear friend, I would like so much for you to be here, with me, tonight to grasp, to share the rapture that I feel just thinking about what I heard this afternoon, and that will sustain me until our concert, and beyond, I hope. Tell me, tell me NOW that you will be present on the 21ST of January!

I am now getting back to work with renewed energy on my music score — for, even if it is not overwhelming, I must play superbly! I will not be unworthy of the confidence our Master has put in me, in all of us, actually!

I will be waiting with the greatest impatience for your dear message. Do not make me weary too long!

> *As always,*
> YOUR CLOTILDE

PARIS, JANUARY 25, 1893

My Eugénie,

Yes, you are right, everything went marvelously well. I am still amazed by it all. The requiem is simply magnificent. People near us are saying that this event will be remembered forever by all who were there. So, I understand why you are so proud of me for having participated in it's success.

And yet, I sense something deeper, more elusive in this euphoria. In fact, in the midst of this success, of this pride that fills me, is a feeling of humility because this beauty created by one man and a few musicians has another dimension: it is, fundamentally, somehow, proof of a divine intervention. Coming from a "good" catholic, this conclusion will not surprise you, but, it is in fact, for me, the only way to explain our enchantment in the *true* sense of the word.

Will I ever again have the good fortune to experience such a moment? Undoubtedly, if I have the opportunity to remain a few months longer among the instrumentalists of our great Fauré. Pray for me, my friend.

And I will do the same for you so that your "friendship" toward Pierre may be fulsomely returned. Speaking of which, have you dared speak to your parents yet about your feelings toward him? Tell me soon.

> *All my tender hugs and kisses,*
> CLO

෬෯

PARIS, FEBRUARY 9, 1893

My most audacious Friend,

I marvel at your ability to convince those around you. Yes, how could your mother possibly refuse to support you when dealing with your father, given all the reasons you gave them so that they would agree to meet your irresistible Pierre?

I feel, just as you do, that your parents will not be unmoved by his charms. But it may rather be his Artesian background, his belonging to the local bourgeoisie and his job in administration that will convince them. So do not worry, because even if your parents did not "find" him, Pierre is exactly the man whom they are seeking for their wonderful daughter. What is more, it is thanks to your uncle that you found him. Which makes me think that this situation is not perhaps just a question of luck. That does not matter. What does matter is that you have the opportunity of becoming the wife of the man with whom you say to be madly in love!

"Madly in love." That expression makes you think that loving someone deeply will lead to madness — which I would not refute, since, basically, what is love? According to our parents, it is a feeling that defies reason, thought, often logic itself and especially prudence. But I want to see in it a path that it supposed to lead us to happiness, true happiness. Do not laugh, and be aware that what is important is that you fully live those moments of joy and happiness. I add my prayers to yours so that everything may go as you wish next Monday. And of course, I wait impatiently for you to tell me in detail just how the meeting will have gone.

YOUR CLOTILDE *(who is thrilled by this whole affair!)*

෴

FRIDAY, APRIL 7, 1893

My dear Eugénie,

What a joy it is to read your letter so full of promises! I can hardly imagine your feelings, your euphoria. Indeed, the fact that your parents have found Pierre to their liking is not surprising, but that they would accept your engagement in three months' time is the most surprising thing!

Our prayers worked, as Mother would say (since she always wants to see the work of the Lord in any happy event).

As for me, no engagement, but much happiness because I am still thrilled by my participation in the masses and other concerts at the Madeleine. Of course that probably does not surprise you. What is more, my work at Blanchet is not too demanding, which lets me work on my scores and coddle my harp with the greatest of pleasure. Of course you know that already. But here is a tidbit that will make you smile: our dinner at the Renaults' last Sunday was most interesting thanks to the vigorous discussions among the three brothers and their friend Jean-Louis Leroy. Yes. Who would ever have guessed that we would see each other again after meeting two years ago in Blois? I would not say that it is a small world, but knowing now that the Leroys are good friends of the Renaults and the Poulains, it is possible that this meeting was not just luck, although Jean-Louis did seem quite surprised (albeit "happy") to see me again. When he was leaving, he said he hoped to invite me to have lunch with some friends at his favorite restaurant, the Zimmer, on Chatelet Square if I would like. We will see if he keeps his word. To tell you the truth, I am rather happy with his proposal.

I will tell you how this new adventure continues, if it does. Meanwhile, give me some details about the great celebration to come.

Your Clo who sends fond kisses

಄

PARIS, SATURDAY, 22 APRIL 1893

My dear Friend, *(Alfred de Berlantier)*

I have to give you some very bad news: Aunt Caroline died yesterday evening around 10 o'clock. Yes, you can imagine our stupor and understand why my letter is so short. A death notice will be sent to you by Monday, but I must give you a few details so that you will be closer to us in your thoughts.

You know that our dear aunt was not doing well this winter and that her health had begun to deteriorate around mid-March. However, despite her persistent cough, we were hoping that she would recover with the coming of good weather. Alas, the Lord had decided otherwise.

The whole family is profoundly upset, but we are concentrating on the arrangements, the death notices, the details for the funeral and the burial, putting off, for a few days, the terrible shock that the loss of those we love brings.

Concerning the funeral, the service will take place in the church of Notre Dame de Grace. According to Aunt Caroline's wishes, we asked that the choir sing the last movement of Berlioz's *Requiem* during the sung mass.

With her departure, an entire generation has disappeared. Despite their disagreements, Mother is very affected because she really admired her aunt: she envied her determination, her optimism, her quiet assurance. All of us, in fact, benefited from the reassuring vision that Aunt Caroline had of the world. She knew how to give us hope when we were distressed or doubted others and ourselves. She was a great lady, to whom I owe much: our encounter among other things.

So much sorrow overwhelms me! Write to me soon, my friend, to console me a little for this cruel loss.

YOUR CLOTILDE

MONDAY, JULY 24, 1893

My sweet Friend,

I am not surprised to learn from you that the celebration of your engagement was such a success. It will also be unforgettable. I await to see the photographs taken on this occasion with great impatience.

I must say that Edouard laughed a lot when I read to him Pierre's commentary, that you reported to me so faithfully, about the splendor of your dinner. Actually, neither my brother nor I have had until now the honor to share lunch with the President of the Chamber of Deputies. So we cannot judge the accuracy of the spontaneous "declaration" which assured your guests that this delicious dinner far surpassed, by the quality of the dishes and the guests, the one offered by Casimir Périer to the very high representatives of our Republic, as you so delightfully say. What is more, I doubt that his wife has a cook comparable to the grand chef of the Chanzy restaurant. Period.

My sadness at not having been with you for this event is compensated by the great success of our concert this past Sunday. But I promise to be present at your wedding no matter what date it is.

I must also say that Mr. de Berlantier and Jean-Louis Leroy (oh yes) were among our many spectators. I will speak to you of this "coincidence" very soon.

> *With all my compliments and my affectionate kisses,*
> CLOTILDE

☙

TUESDAY, AUGUST 1, 1893

My dear, dear Eugénie,

I promised to "light your lantern" concerning the presence of Mr. de Berlantier and of Jean-Louis Leroy at our concert last week. Do not worry: I am not the monkey of Mr. de Florian,[4] even though I love his fable and, of course, the song. Well, it appears that these two gentlemen have known each other for years thanks to their mutual friends, the Renaults and the d'Argis. What is more, Alfred de Berlantier is very interested in the mechanical work that Jean-Louis pursues, having the same passion for automobiles, which brought him close to the Renault son. Furthermore, my cousins are related to the de Berlantiers through their Jurassian roots, and Jean-Louis, as you know, is a native of the Loire valley region, as are the Renaults. That is right! You see how much the haute bourgeoisie and the petite nobility come together in our wonderful capital. The presence of these two men at our concert is thus not surprising.

But to get to what really interests you: I do not see any conflict about my relationship with these two men, because they occupy a very different place in my life and in my heart! Alfred for me is a friend, a support, a counselor. I think he feels some affection for me, but nothing more that I can detect. If his feelings are deeper, he hides them well! I believe in fact that he may consider me like a younger sister, as he is 15 years older than I am. The reasons for these sentiments are not clear, but I am not going to ask him to explain their origins, as I do not want to receive an answer that would embarrass me . . .

As for Jean-Louis, you know well that, just like you, I thought I had forgotten about our little fling. Two years ago already! Yes, we were quite innocent: it was our first grand ball, our first step towards "high" society, and our first trip to the beautiful city of Blois (and the only one until now). It was also the discovery of our powers of seduction . . . Those young men were so charming and attentive that we were quite taken at first sight, and it was easy for us to believe their compliments. However, we were sensible enough to resist their clear, though unspoken, desire. And this good behavior allowed you to become the happy wife of your adorable Pierre. As for me, I am free to take matters up where I left off, but without the taboos and the limits imposed by our parents and our fears. Will I go beyond a loving friendship with this very charming man if such is his desire? I think so, and why not? Perhaps he will want to take me as his wife? Meanwhile, I remain reserved and maintain the distance required by propriety.

So, my dear friend, there is how things stand. Have I satisfied your curiosity? We will talk about all of this when you come to Paris on September 2ND: things will be, perhaps, a little clearer for me, too, by then. And there is no need to say how impatient I am to see you.

I will leave you to get back to my work: the drawing of a harmonious bouquet of wildflowers that I need to send to Furnion Company before the end of the week.

Your Clo, who hugs you tight

☙

My very dear Friend,

I have to tell you, or rather share with you, my own experience concerning the event that all the newspapers are talking about today. I am sure you guessed it: the "national" funeral of Charles Gounod! You will not be surprised to learn that our church opened its doors wide to celebrate that glorious musician. Do you remember our pleasure when we listened to his *Messe à la mémoire de Jeanne d'Arc* together at the church of St. Eustache, four years ago? How sad that he has left us so soon — well, not really so soon since people say he was already 75 years old!

But he must be reassured for his works are here, safely kept on their scores. The musician's work may disappear after each concert (even if it remains in our memories), while the composer's work will survive assuredly! Just like the painter's work thanks to his canvases! Perhaps that is why I am so taken by drawing . . .

But back to today. Imagine, my dear Eugénie, just imagine a church filled to capacity, an unbelievable quantity of magnificent flowers, a most solemn mass, Saint-Saëns at the great organ and Fauré masterfully directing the choir. Imagine, the beautiful service by our priest, whose voice has such an uncommon musicality. A most vibrant Gregorian Mass for the Dead. And then, imagine three of the most moving eulogies given by important persons whom we so admire in the world of Arts: Jean-Léon Gérôme, Ambroise Thomas, still president of the Conservatory, and finally Saint-Saëns himself, since he was apparently a great friend of Gounod. Imagine the audience, first fascinated, then transported by "our" Requiem at the end of the mass. Yes, who would ever have thought that we would have the pleasure of playing it again this year and in this place! It was one of the most beautiful and very touching moments.

It is too bad that it took a funeral, full of tears and sadness, to experience those magnificent moments! You would point out that requiems are composed, in fact, to give the dead the rest that they deserve, and also to console the living . . .

So there you have, my friend, an explanation for my state of mind; furthermore, a little dinner, Monday night at the Zimmer restaurant with Jean-Louis, might well explain my good spirits. But I will tell you all about that in a few days, as I will see him again at the end of the week.

Many kisses,
Your Clo

૯৲৩

My Eugénie,

What a pleasure to have spent two beautiful days in your company! I hope that your grandmother did not feel too abandoned. She must understand that the rarer your visits in Paris are, the more they should be shared with those who love you! And there are many of us.

Thank you also for the details about my voyage to Arras. Arriving on the 17TH seems like a good idea: that way I'll have a little time to get adjusted as you so nicely put it . . . I should tell you that I really appreciate being one of your bridesmaids. I will do my best to fulfill this duty the way I should.

Mother finished the last little touches on my dress yesterday evening. Edouard came in and said, in the most admiring tone, that I should be posing for Charles Frederick Worth. Mother told him that I was not a "look-alike" and that fashion shows certainly lead to prostitution.

She obviously does not appreciate these fashion experts, and the heavy hand they have on a profession which, until now, belonged mostly to women.

But I have to get this letter to the post office before six o'clock, for January 19TH will be here soon, even if it seems so long given our impatience.

A thousand big kisses,
CLOTILDE

૯৲৩

My dear Auguste,

It has been a long time since we have had any news from

you, and your parents seem not to have had much either. So, tell use soon how your life is in that gray city of London.

On this side of the Channel, things are going rather well. Edouard is busy finishing the last chair to the dining room set of which you admired his original and careful work. Mother is very proud of the talents of her son and is impatient to invite the whole family around the beautiful table which, with its two leaves, will easily seat ten people. For me, the most remarkable thing is the simplicity of the sideboard doors which highlight the beauty of the oak: no complicated sculptures, but very precise work of raised squares. He also worked hard on the feet of the table, even though table feet rarely call one's attention. But you know Edouard's taste for perfection . . .

Apart from that, nothing new in his life or mine, although I am very busy. After my long days at Blanchet, I help Mother as much as I can because she is a little tired. Still, I set aside several evenings to work, with great pleasure, on my designs. I have, in fact, several orders from Furnion Company. But be at ease: I do not ignore my harp!

I must tell you also that you may be assured: I upheld my role as maid of honor at Eugénie's wedding. It was a magnificent event, and I did not fall into the arms of the best man who had been assigned to me; fear not!

Our young couple have just returned from a wonderful honeymoon in Italy. I will show you photos and post cards once you return to Paris, you who so much love Italy. Meanwhile, I must get back to work; I leave you then while wishing you an interesting week and many serious clients who appreciate, as they should, the beautiful French furniture that you offer them. OR that you have on offer

Mother joins me in sending you big hugs.

CLOTILDE

ℰ↷

My very dear Friend,

I read your letter with great pleasure, especially since you now seem to be well settled into your beautiful house in Arras. I am also thrilled to know that Pierre is keeping his position at the prefecture, even if I would have preferred that you move to Paris. Perhaps that will be possible in a year or two.

But you know all of that. So I am going to talk to you about something else. First of all, thank you, thank you a thousand times for your superb photos and post cards; they have allowed me to follow you in your wonderful honeymoon trip! I only wish that one day I too will be able to send you cards from the places that I will explore with the man of my dreams. That thought leads me to tell you a few words about recent events concerning my relationship with Jean-Louis.

He comes faithfully to wait for me when I leave the Madeleine church after our late afternoon rehearsals. Then he takes me either to the beautiful tea house on the Madeleine Square that offers delicious cakes, if it is not yet 7:00, or to a little calm and elegant restaurant on Tronchet Street to have dinner. We chat about this and that, we share our thoughts and ideas on the events of the day. He talks to me about his life, about his passion for mechanics; I describe to him my designs, the trends in fashion, but I remain evasive about what I want and how I see the future. And above all, I do not ask him any questions about the destiny of our relationship. In fact, we are "learning" each other, if I may say so. I must confess that I appreciate his reserve, as much as his attentions.

So there you see where I am, for the time being. But I must

leave you to help Mother: we are expecting my cousins, the Guyots, who will be joining us for dinner.

> *I wish you both a magnificent month of May*
> *and I send you many hugs,*
> CLOTILDE

PARIS, JUNE 15, 1894

My dear Eugénie,

Just a quick word to tell you that yesterday your grandmother shared with me your wonderful news. Bravo, bravo!

She told me how happy she was that you and Pierre are embarked on this path right now because she will be able to have "the great pleasure of meeting the little one before leaving us!" Actually she seems to me to be in good health and does not show her age, which makes me think that she will still be here well after the month of December . . . I must admit to being very touched by her enthusiasm, which I share! Even though I do not see myself in your situation — not being the wife of your adorable husband! In fact, I am sure that you and Pierre are very happy about your condition, even if a pregnancy is not always easy to go through. I wish you, therefore, very good health for the next six months, and I am thrilled to see you both in two short weeks.

I am leaving to go to the Drouot Hotel where I am going to "guide" my friend Alfred de Berlantier.

I do not know if you have heard of the passing of Philippe Parrot, this excellent portraitist, a month ago now. His works will be sold at auction this afternoon. Alfred wants to buy a few, and seeks my advice.

It should be a most interesting afternoon. I do not doubt that yours will be any less so!

> *Hugs to both of you, very affectionately,*
> YOUR CLOTILDE

☙

MONDAY, OCTOBER 1ST, 1894

My dear Friend, (Alfred de Berlantier)

What a lovely evening! How you spoiled me! The dinner at the Grand Véfour was simply divine! I am still amazed at the taste of those delicious dishes, the elegance of the restaurant, the impeccable demeanor of the maître d'hôtel! And the beautiful flowers that you so generously provided for the ladies at our table, as to be forgiven the extra attention that you paid me!

I must also mention the brilliant conversation that you managed so adroitly. But something else preoccupies me at the moment. In effect, I promised our good priest to speak to you of the repairs to be done, in all haste, to the trumpeter angel that adorns the upper part of the organ in our Church of the Madeleine. As you know, a great concert is to take place, and we want everything to be resplendent to honor our great Massenet.

Yes, you read it correctly; it appears that Fauré has decided that we will play three works of the grand Master, including the *Symphony in F* and several passages of *Thais*, notably the "Meditation." You will remember the joy we felt in hearing this magnificent opera last March. And how I was moved to tears, of course at the death of Thais, but above all during the "Meditation!" I have not failed since to play this piece written for violin and harp nearly every day! It has a magical effect on my fingers and wrists: it puts me in a state of grace, and my rehearsal work feels lightened, effortless!

But let us return to my concerns: the wounded angel.
Yes, a part of the left wing was damaged by a falling piece
of the cornice last winter. It should, no it MUST, with the
utmost urgency, be repaired, re-gilded to give it back its
original luster. Our church is rather dark; the brightness of
its gilding is essential to reflect the sparse light of the candles.
But, you may ask, what do I have to do with all that? Well,
it happens that the sculptor in charge of these repairs is my
cousin, Alexandre Guyot. He is a very talented wood carver,
trained by my grandfather Théophile. Furthermore, despite
his undeniable talent, he is not expensive and is willing to
undertake this restoration right away. This, obviously, suits our
priest, since the city and the archbishop are dragging their
feet. However, Alexandre could undertake the work only if
we get him the necessary scaffolding. And that is where you
come in. Indeed, it seems to me that your friend, Pierre de
la Montagne, was the one to provide the scaffolding used by
the crew of Charles Joseph Lameire during the placement of
the mosaic in the chancel ceiling. I remember being afraid
for the poor man when he decided to climb up to inspect the
work of his mosaicists! Can you imagine yourself at 62, way
up above the main altar, magnifying glass in hand, examining
the joints between the little blue or gold squares? But, the
scaffold being well constructed, the old man felt at ease in
the rarefied air, and was able to come down without difficulty
after his inspection. All that to say how reassured I would be if
your Monsieur de la Montagne could erect the scaffold, which
would be, by the way, much lower than the one erected for
Lameire. This would permit Alexandre — not such a young
man anymore since he must be about 46 years old — to
complete the work rapidly.

And of course, as I well know your generosity, I know that
you will want to plead with your friend so that his participation

in this good work will be not too expensive, if not free. Is it too much to count on your support? Is it too much to ask of you who are always ready to please me? Furthermore, is it not a very good cause?

Oh, my friend, do not mock me! You know how attached I am to this church! But you may not know that my feelings are anchored in the memory of my family. You see, my grandfather, who was a wood sculptor before becoming a piano maker, left his mark in this church, since he worked on the decoration of the pulpit and the stalls. You must know that the chancel furniture was completed at the beginning of the forties, when the Loevens were still very sought out among the craftsmen of the Faubourg Saint-Antoine.

So, my Friend, that is all I ask. You now know what would bring me the most pleasure. Admit that it is not exorbitant! In addition, I am giving you, when you consider it, the chance to serve our church, so close to God. That is how our souls can improve their slight chance to go to Heaven, one day . . .

> *Your devoted and so appreciative*
> CLOTILDE

ॐ

SATURDAY, NOVEMBER 17, 1894

My sweet Friend,

I hope that this nasty storm on Monday did not cause too much damage in Arras. The newspapers are talking about all those uprooted trees, lifted roofs, and steeples that lost their roosters.[5] So I was really afraid for you and want you to reassure me as soon as possible!

Nature is decidedly cruel, when one considers the floods that paralyzed Artois last month! What should we expect from the cold months of the coming winter? But we must be optimistic and imagine the beautiful things that await us. I am thinking, of course, of the birth of your child.

That brings me to another topic: my coming to Arras. I cannot leave Paris next week because I am participating in a little concert on Tuesday the 27TH. In addition, Saturday the first seems too close to your due date. It seems wiser to me to push back my visit till after Christmas. What do you think? Rest assured that I am very eager to see you, but I must also be reasonable — Mother would be very proud to hear me say such things to you!

I presume also that you are very busy making the room ready for the precious one who will be filling your life; my absence will thus be less difficult to accept unless I am mistaken.

Tell me also the results of the steps Pierre has taken with his superiors concerning his long overdue promotion. A little justice would not be bad for anyone in this world where iniquity seems to reign.

I must close now so that this letter may go out tonight. I am enclosing a few drawings to cheer you up and to bring a bit of sunshine to the still gray skies of Arras.

Take good care of yourself, of you both, my sweet friend.

> *I hug you with a little regret but lots of affection,*
> CLOTILDE

⁂

PARIS, MONDAY, DECEMBER 10, 1894

My very dear Friend,

I just learned from your mother that little Simone was born without much difficulty, and that you are both in excellent health. We are all thrilled by this good news and wish you a speedy recovery.

What a beautiful time for you and Pierre, and for the whole

family! Your mother is so happy that she laughed while telling me that "the men of the family were hoping, as is proper, for a boy," but that you would "be able to please them next time!" Well, a boy. We need at least one, and the firstborn if possible, because he will carry the name and the family fortune. We women can only lose our maiden name; and our dowries drain the funds that are so necessary to our brothers!

For my part, I have another reason to compliment you: your mother stressed that you have decided to nurse the baby yourself, in spite of the expected decency that your "ladies in waiting" did not hesitate to recall to you. Me, of course, I applaud your decision for reasons that are not unfamiliar to you: my mother has always blamed herself for having placed my older sister with a wet-nurse in La Ferté-Gaucher, while she could have nursed her herself, even if it meant using a bottle when needed. But I am certain that you have discussed all that with the women around you; so I will stop and simply tell you to fully enjoy those precious moments, and too bad if your social life is not as full: there will always be dinners and balls next year where you will shine.

What is more, if you want to reassure your family on the validity of your decision, you can remind them that Queen Marie-Antoinette, sensitive to the arguments of Jean-Jacques Rousseau, was completely in favor of maternal nursing since she had persuaded the king to give a little pension to those young Parisian wives who nursed their babies. Who could argue with a queen? And, as everyone knows, she was the first to preside over the Society for Maternal Charity, followed by all our empresses! And that is without mentioning our patronesses today, of whom your mother is one! Well, I shall stop here, because you have more to do than read my ramblings . . .

While waiting to meet this precious little being who is going to fill your sweet life, I am sending today a little present to

celebrate her arrival. I cannot tell you how impatient I am to
take her in my arms . . .

> *I affectionately send hugs and kisses to*
> *the three of you,*
> YOUR CLO

THURSDAY, FEBRUARY 14, 1895

My dear Eugénie,

Your letter filled with so much good news arrived this
morning; it gave me such pleasure that I must write back
before the last mail goes out!

Indeed, your friendship warms my heart, which is quite
useful with such cold weather! In fact, and to answer your
first question, it was 5°F at noon today in our courtyard. My
brother told me last night that, according to experts in meteo-
rology (what a pretty word!), the average temperature in Paris
has not been so low for 150 years. It must be the same in
Arras! That is definitely something to worry about.

I must tell you also that I was quite surprised, going by the
Place du Châtelet last night, to see huge thick sheets of ice
suspended from the sphinxes' mouths at the fountain. It is such
an unbelievable sight that all the passers-by stop and stare in
spite of the intense cold! As for the Seine, frozen to such a
great depth: as you might imagine, a crowd of young people
have the great pleasure of crossing it on "dry" foot! I suspect
that the Scarpe, too, is attracting a large number of youths (be
they skaters or not).

Still, the interruption of river transport is a source of
worry not only for merchants, but for all of us, as I am sure
you realize. In fact, the price of wood and coal has suddenly
increased, which dismays many people around me, my
mother first of all. She now puts so little wood in our pretty

Salamander stove that it is almost cold in our apartment, to the point that I am keeping on my woolen gloves, even to write you . . .

But what gives me some consolation, and which will make you smile, is the silver fox set (fur collar and muff) that Jean-Louis gave me as this New Year's gift; a much appreciated gift that goes elegantly with my long, gray wool coat (the one whose cut you so admired), and protects me whenever I have to face the persistent cold outside, and inside, too!

That leads me to answer your question: where is my relationship with Jean-Louis going? I must admit that I do not know exactly how to unravel all the confused feelings that torment me. I really enjoy the affection of this generous, charming man, but I am not sure I can promise to go further. In spite of my admiration for him, something holds me back, a sort of ill-defined fear. Much as I would like us to share a lasting relationship, because I do have some deep feelings for him, I just cannot bring myself to believe in happiness. A happiness like yours. Actually, I often think of your relationship with Pierre, of the clarity of your feelings: you knew from the first day that he was the man destined for you. I am far from any assurance such as yours, but still I think I will never love another man as much. But who knows? Let's hope that in a few months' time things will be both clearer and more satisfying.

But let us talk a little about you, your life as wife and mother, such a rich, significant, admirable life, and I could go on . . . Your choices surprise me and thrill me. Indeed, how do you decide? Abandoning your numerous activities to dedicate yourself to be a wife; nursing your child yourself rather than employing a wet-nurse; encouraging Pierre to take a post in Africa while you are so attached to your family, and I am not even mentioning your role as a choir member, which you will have to relinquish. I would call that devotion: a devotion without limits, praiseworthy! You might tell me again and again that this is the love of a wife, of a mother. However, does that love so easily erase your own needs, your desires, your talents? That is the mystery of love, a mystery that scares me a little, I must confess, and which I do not really see myself knowing one day . . .

Before leaving you, I want to tell you how happy I am that your little Simone is no longer interrupting your short nights too often. That you can fall asleep while she is at your breast speaks volumes about the ease with which you play your role of mother. Pierre, as much as you, must appreciate this respite and no longer doubt your decision to nurse your little angel yourself. A well-rested mother, according to my mother, is more likely to produce a rich and delicious milk . . . Enjoy this wonderful pleasure!

Edouard has offered to post my letter since he has to go over to the Bastille. So I will stop here, wishing you, and of course your adorable family, a pleasant and relaxing end of the week in spite of this very cold spell which surely will not last much longer.

> *A thousand big kisses,*
>
> CLO

P.S.: You know how the verb "employ" is so popular these days. It is not that I am falling into the yoke of fashion; but the use of this verb should not be limited to the activities or the world of men. A wet-nurse is paid for her services, as much as is a blacksmith or a pastry chef; she is therefore employed!

This little postscript says much about my unyielding position, which, my Eugénie, cannot surprise you.

THURSDAY, MARCH 7, 1895

My dear Eugénie,

My silence must be worrying you, so I hasten to respond to your letter of February 20TH, which, as always, gave me great pleasure.

So here is my story, which is neither cheerful nor very original. A week ago, I slipped while descending the steps of the small Clotilde de Vaux Street, which connects Beaumarchais Boulevard to Amiot Street. I was hoping to quickly reach Chemin Vert Street. But I found myself lying on the sidewalk, unable to get up, my left shoulder and elbow twisted and my wrist quite painful. Two kindly gentlemen helped me to stand up, but I had to take a hackney coach to return home — so a goodly portion of my pin money is now gone! Still, I must reassure you: the bonesetter who has put our little family to rights for two generations has assured me that, thanks to his good care, the bones of my shoulder and elbow have been put back in place, but the joints will remain painful for a week or two. The swelling in my wrist will go down if I apply cold (which is not difficult these days!) and the bruising on my leg will quickly disappear.

Today the aching in my wrist and the bruises are still there. Moreover, my elbow has not totally regained its flexibility, but I remain optimistic because I am making progress. I continue to work at Blanchet, and I can draw without too much difficulty, in spite of my immobilized left hand, and thanks in large part to the genius of Edouard who showed me how to put weights on my sheets of paper so that they do not move when I am working with pencils or brushes.

Nonetheless, the consequences of my fall are fairly alarming because it is impossible at the present to play my harp. You can imagine my anxiety! I immediately informed our Chapel Master. Fauré being very busy at the conservatory, François

Manson, who often assists him, quickly located another harpist to replace me. I hope to rejoin the musicians and the choir as soon as possible, but as you know so well, "patience and time . . ." I am living that saying.

I must add that my "affliction" is bringing me some unexpected attention from my friends. Jean-Louis in particular. He sends me flowers and sweets so often that I do not know where to put them, being, as it should be, not very fond of sweets. Perhaps that is all going to change . . .

Well, there you have, my dear, the most important news. Tell me what is happening in Arras, your few outings, and the progress of your little angel. When will you know for certain if your father will obtain again a position in Paris? Soon, I hope!

Your Clo who hugs you and wishes you all good
health with no falls, no worries . . .

❧

My very dear Friend,

Your letter, which arrived this morning, is such a beautiful reason for me to celebrate spring and to forget my worries! Especially because the news that you share warms my heart! In fact, I cannot believe that your little baby of a mere three months has already learned to smile at you, that she prefers to take your hand rather than the maid's, that she responds to your arpeggios! All of that points to the vivacity of her mind, her easiness in a world so new to her; it is all so deeply moving, and makes me even a little envious . . . Shall I ever know such happiness? I doubt it because it comes with a price! Let us just say that my admiration for you and Pierre has no limits. My only request is that you continue to describe those delicious moments so that I, too, may taste them!

In the meantime, let me answer your question: my progress until now has not been very fast; my elbow remains painful, but I am finally able to move my wrist from left to right without too much pain, which is reassuring. Anyway, according to the bonesetter, I will regain (and I quote): "All the flexibility of my elbow and my wrist in one or two weeks depending on the weather!" This last detail is a little unsettling; while it is much less cold than it was in February, the gray skies of Paris are not a cause for optimism.

But who knows? My state of mind not depending solely on nice weather, my recovery may very well come to be thanks to the *nice* moments that life affords me these days. Yes, I confess to having spent a magnificent day yesterday with Jean-Louis. It went like this: we met around 11 o'clock at Saint-Germain-des-Prés in that little restaurant next to Les Deux-Magots, which you no doubt recall. After a light lunch, we went to the Salon des Cent, quite close by, on Bonaparte Street, in the building that houses *La Plume*, the review that sets all Paris abuzz with its avant-gardism and its alluring covers. In fact, the cover on this month's issue shows two beautiful young women representing the arts and literature; it is a cover designed by Eugene Grasset himself! Of course I religiously keep all the issues of this review, as you might well imagine.

As for the exposition at the Salon des Cent, which is held in the entrance to *La Plume*, I must say that I was quite surprised by both the quantity and the quality of the works by painters, sculptors, engravers and lithographers that one can purchase at quite a low price, according to Jean-Louis. I really loved the engravings and drawings by Alphonse Mucha. Jean-Louis thinks that he is too influenced perhaps by the works of Grasset: languorous women whose arms and hands are too evident; serious faces; long, luxurious hair; a great profusion of flowers, plants or trees. After our very nice visit, we left with a lithograph by Pierre Bonnard and a poster by Jules Chéret; two names that may not mean much to you, but according to Jean-Louis, will soon be quite famous! I would have liked a poster by Mucha, but that will have to wait. And of course when you come to Paris, I will take you to that most interesting place!

So now you know how your Clo spends a little of her time now that she can no longer, for the time being, caress her harp!

She also thinks about you all and sends many hugs.
CLOTILDE

⸎

TUESDAY, JUNE 11, 1895

My very dear Friend,

Thank you for your letter and for all the wonderful news about your little Simone — what an angel!

As for my "condition," I must say that all your wishes for my recovery have been successful, since I am now in a much better state! A state that allows me to get back to work on my music with energy these last ten days, and that without overly fatiguing my wrist or my elbow. You would think I would be, therefore, full of enthusiasm. But, no, and here is why.

Feeling ready to face the world, I went to the Madeleine Sunday for high mass. I was able to admire the work of the choir and the instrumentalists. But that is where my euphoria stops. Indeed, when I approached François Manson, the organist of the smaller organ who lately has often been replacing Fauré as the head of the choir, he told me quite simply that the person who replaced me the day after my unwelcome fall, is particularly gifted. Moreover, she has a License from the Philharmonic University, which makes her a better candidate than I am to permanently replace Madame Nastelle (who died three months ago now). The final decision will be made before the end of the month when our gentlemen will be able to meet. I had the impression, incorrectly perhaps, that he was personally taken by this young, so very "talented," harpist.

You are right to tell me: "Who are you to insinuate such nonsense, you who benefited from Berlantier's influence with Fauré?" And you would be correct, for I must admit that my presence among the instrumentalists is not due to my exceptional talents alone!

That twaddle must reassure you on my state of mind, as, although very saddened, I see a little hope thanks to Mother. In fact, after listening to my diatribe, she told me quite simply: "Adversity makes us stronger. Take advantage of this little misfortune to forge ahead. Moreover, there are many other orchestras and groups in and around Paris, and your three years at the Madeleine will give you an excellent advantage." Of course, she is not wrong.

So, my friend, there you have my little inconveniences. Sharing them with you gives me both courage and determination. So I am going to take Mother's advice and speak to those around me to find some other musical options. Moreover, I am really working hard on my designs and play my harp as often as I can. On the other hand, as I have told you, Jean-Louis takes me for nice walks and pampers me so: should I regret not having fallen earlier? I call upon your profound understanding of people to enlighten me on this unexpected aspect of my love life. Meanwhile, I send hugs to all three of you, and hope to hear from you soon.

Your Clo

PARIS, SEPTEMBER 10, 1895

My dear Auguste,

Many thanks for your letter which is so reassuring. Is it not curious that your broken leg, following your "unfortunate" fall, has allowed you to remain in Algeria and not go do battle in Madagascar? Is it not a gift from heaven? Undoubtedly, for, according to the Paris papers, the French troops and the African Regiment in particular, have lost many men these last few weeks. So stay as long as possible in the calm city of Blida, your detailed description of which was much appreciated by us all. Thank you also for the photograph of the camp where you reside: the great plain and the little sandy hills are quite different from the mountainous and forested countrysides of Madagascar that you so wanted to see, but is your curiosity worth your life?

Furthermore, in spite of your optimism, it is not at all certain that our army can take Tananarive and impose a protectorate upon Queen Ranavalona. Anyway, I do not really understand the need to impose our presence on this people who are so different from us and yet so admirable from many points of view. And where does our politicians' enthusiasm for conquests come from? Are there not other ways to make our France a "great" country, a nation respected and respectable, a place where it is *truly* good to live?

I have another thought that needs your opinion: you could have done your military service in Poitiers or even in Versailles, where the life of a soldier, be in the cavalry or no, should not be too difficult for a young Parisian who until now has been fascinated by the arts of woodworking and furniture. So, is your posting based on something other than your love of travel and adventure? And if so, are you satisfied with it? I am not at all convinced that this was a good choice on the part of a young cousin whom I thought I knew.

But let us move on to your questions about our little life in Paris. Understand that it is rather precarious these days. First, an unexpected heat wave (93° F yesterday) has made almost any activity difficult. And the drought (no rain since August 14) is affecting the parks and gardens in an alarming way, especially the smaller market gardeners: no water for the vegetables that are their sole source of income. There is very little potable water in some neighborhoods, and a great number of drinking fountains have already dried up. In our courtyard, the well is not yet dry, but for how long? Only a short while, undoubtedly. "It is unheard of!" as Mother says.

Who would ever have expected such heat after the extreme cold of February? Life is becoming more and more difficult for ordinary people! And our prayers go unanswered. We hardly go out of the house and keep the shutters closed. Edouard works very early in the morning and late at night, but rests during the day, like most of the artisans in the area.

In spite of it all, the sideboard whose "birth" you saw, is almost finished; you will be impressed by the quality of our sculptor's work. Who would ever have thought that so much talent might be in our family? I must say that Edouard learned a great deal during his ten years' apprenticeship, from your father and his generosity!

Mother and I sew little because our clients are not thinking ahead to next winter, given the heat that is paralyzing us all. We therefore spend our little pocket money parsimoniously. But I still have the pleasure of designing a little and of working a lot on my music as I hope to rejoin the musicians of Saint-Eustache next month: my three years at the Madeleine ought to work in my favor.

Jean-Louis has left for Mulhouse for the burial of an aged cousin: a welcome trip since it is cooler in the East than in

Paris, and the cousin (she was quite old) has proven to be very generous toward him.

So there you have it, my dear Auguste, all that I can tell you for today. I am sorry not to have more interesting or funny things to share. I will try harder next time, when life in Paris will have resumed its gaiety, thanks to cooler, rainier weather!

Tell us soon whether you will be able to have a leave to come to Paris before the end of the year.

Many hugs,
CLOTILDE

ॐ

PARIS, JANUARY 13, 1896

My dear Auguste,

Your letter was much appreciated, and we are quite happy to know that you are in good health and are satisfied with your time in the African Regiment. We send you all our best wishes that it may continue. Those wishes are even more heartfelt and profound since we so enjoyed your brief visit in early December. Mother is particularly grateful, as she does so love your parents. They are very sensitive, warm, compassionate people; we always feel at ease in their company — and in yours, too, of course! Mother often says that we are fortunate to have you for a cousin. And Edouard and I feel the same!

Speaking of cousins, I should tell you that Henri is not doing well. He has been deeply shaken by the sudden death, last Tuesday, of Verlaine whose health had been very bad for several months; but Henri, although a doctor, refused to see reality. After the burial Friday, he came by the house, which he does only rarely; but I think he needed to share his grief. Since Mother was at a client's house, I had the "honor" of conversing with him for a long while. He is really an extraordinary thinker, and his vision of the world, albeit sometimes extravagant, as you have so often said, is not so far distant from that of our Guyot grand-parents.

Still, I understand his distress, as Verlaine played an import-ant role in his "artist's" life, in particular having written a very positive introduction for Henri's first book (which was quite controversial). But what I found really touching was his profound admiration for Verlaine. He said several times how this poet, so little respected in today's literary world, will undoubtedly be considered one of the greatest poets of the century. As I dared express a few doubts, he recited, in his melodious voice, two short poems that moved me deeply. And now I really want to read all of Verlaine's works! I must also say that his *Cinq mélodies "de Venise"* which Fauré set to music, are remarkable. Anyway, I am now convinced, and our Henri seemed to feel somewhat better when he left. But I think he would appreciate a little word from you.

It is time I leave you now, as it will take me longer than usual to get to Saint-Eustache (to participate with "dignity" in our rehearsal), the streetcars being packed due to the persistent cold. You are lucky to be in Africa!

I will write again soon to talk to you about the chapel master and of my progress in this choir that has been the most wel-coming to me.

> *Your cousin who sends a big hug,*
> CLO

Dear Cousins,

I hope that you are in good health and excellent spirits. Just in case you might be a little morose, I am going to bring you some news that will astonish you as much as it will amuse you. Are you ready?

My sweet brother, our big-hearted artist has just found a new job. So far nothing surprising since cabinet-making is not very well paid these days, due to the arrival of so many Alsatian artists and craftsmen . . . you know a bit about this. Edouard needed an occupation that suited his training, his age, and his desire to stay near us — he is still the support of our family. So he sent in an application, and got the job! But you will never guess what kind of job, nor where it is. I will help you out: he wears a handsome uniform. Have you guessed? No, he has not joined the infantry or artillery — as you know he never really liked the life of a soldier in Orleans, despite the uniform.

He started work a week ago, not far from our rue Saint-Bernard, in fact only a few steps from the Bastille. Can you imagine? No, he is not a fireman in the beautiful new station boulevard Diderot that you like, even if his height would have made him an excellent firefighter. Have you guessed at last? Yes? No? He is now *a police officer*! Are you surprised? Are you giggling like I did, but up your sleeve? I must admit I needed a lot of control to keep from laughing out loud when he told us of his dealings with the municipal authorities. So, now you know! But do not make fun of him, he deserves our support instead: he did it so he could offer us a stable and adequate financial support.

We may of course be surprised at his choice, given his pleasant personality, his funny and good-natured side. But if we look closely we can see that his choice is not that startling: Edouard has always been careful to obey orders — that made him a good apprentice — and he is rather authoritarian with his family and friends. Mother, who believes completely in family influence, sees nothing surprising: her grandfather Ansart was a commissaire in Epinal for many years and our great-uncle Charles spent a few years as a gendarme. On the side of the Loeven, there are at least two gendarmes, including the father of our cousin Davaillau. So much for family tradition; and that is not counting the soldiers. In short, according to Mother, we have no reason to be surprised. Nonetheless, I find it hard to imagine him beneath his kepi, he who up to now was so elegant and so gallant with the ladies.

Write to me about your latest doings; tell me about your life in Lumbres, now that our dear aunt and uncle are no longer there. I admit that I miss them a lot, above all the art of good conversation they shared so well. *Your affectionate Clotilde*

P.S.: I am enclosing a very "martial" photo of our new police officer.

Oh, my dear Friend, (Jean-Louis Leroy)

I too must write about this terrible event since you are not here to discuss it with me.[6] You see, I need to speak about it. I need to put my thoughts in order, share them with you, a man of compassion.

You undoubtedly read the newspapers, in spite of your busy schedule. They are going off the deep end with sensational pictures and upsetting articles about the victims. I heard that the *Petit Journal Illustré* printed 120,000 copies yesterday, but there was not a single one to be found by noon, in all of Paris! Have we all turned suddenly so compassionate, or are we simply fascinated by the misfortune of others? Frankly, do we need these heart-breaking images to think about these children, these women, all those who were gathered in this alley to help a good cause, and are now paying, not only with their lives, but also with excruciating pain and suffering?

If we are seeking gory details, is it to strengthen our compassion? Or are we simply fascinated by the sensational aspect of the catastrophe? All these rich and famous people caught in a fire . . . And those figures, are they even true? Twelve hundred visitors at this Charity Bazar, that day, in that little place — not much more than a twelve hundred square foot alley, in the rue Jean Goujon? Really? This seems to me way too much! As for the victims, according to my brother, their number has reached one hundred and thirty deaths so far, and more than two hundred injured, some so seriously that they are expected to die very soon . . . But if these numbers were lower, would we feel less shaken by the fate of these victims? I certainly hope not!

What is attracting my attention is the fact that, among these victims, we count at least 123 women and children! This raises

Letters from Clotilde

a very embarrassing question: how did the men escape the fire? The answer is simple and quite disturbing: they escaped by pushing aside, and even trampling, women and children! Yes, we shiver at the thought of this unforgivable conduct, this unparalleled cowardice and selfishness! And to think that all these gentlemen belong to the Parisian upper-class, the French High Society, the European ruling class! Of course, before casting the stone, we all must ask ourselves: "What would I have done in such circumstances?" I dare not answer, but you, my friend? You, I know, would have acted in the right way! Yes, I am imagining you in this inferno, making your way through the fleeing crowds to lead them safely toward the doors. I can see you rushing back to rescue the terrified children and the ladies tangled up in their muslin dresses, panic stricken.

Am I wrong? Please do not tell me! I do not want to doubt everything and everyone. I must absolutely believe in the reality of human dignity, in our need to transcend our self-centeredness, in our deep sense of honor. We absolutely cannot accept this every-man-for-himself tendency, this obvious indifference and most destructive selfishness. So I pray, not only for the victims, but also for us all, for our very souls. For there is more: you will see that this catastrophe will be used to put its occurrence on the so-called anarchists or Dreyfus' friends, or the socialists: all those who have somewhat criticized the upper bourgeoisie and the aristocracy lately. Others will mock our religion and will sneer like the heathens they are, denying the existence of God in view of these tragedies. Oh! Politics!

In the streets, people shake their head to show their empathy with the victims, but is this feeling of compassion going to last? Is it going to breach the gap separating our social classes in a durable fashion, torn as we are by the memory of 1871?[7] I doubt it, as resentment can continue under those forced

84

smiles. You see, in my neighborhood, the pains inflicted on the Communards are far from being forgotten . . . So I pray for more forgiveness among the various groups of the Paris population.

Yes, I am praying while others are in non-stop motion: the journalists are breaking loose; the newspaper owners are making a fortune; our leaders are looking hastily for the culprits, and spend much time and energy in ceremoniously rewarding firemen and policemen; our priests celebrate mass after mass; our engineers are finally trying to imagine more efficient water pumps — Yes, Mr. Krebs is proposing automatic pumps powered by electric current (progress never stops), but where was he two days ago? As for the reason of the fire: the film was running too close to the projector lamp. Well, you would expect a quick proposal, right away, from our engineers to improve the projection system. But no! From now on, public cinematic performances are forbidden — a perfect way to avoid fires! The authority has spoken. So you see, lots of actions, but little reflection.

Yes, little action, and no memory! Eight years ago, in January and February, a flu outbreak killed more than four hundred and fifty people, PER DAY, in Paris. Little was done at the time to stop the epidemic that could start again next winter. But we do not think about it anymore. We make no connection at all between disasters.

What is missing also in this chaos, are the comforting words, and the will to find efficient ways to bring solace to the victims and their families. Where is the reassurance that their suffering has any value? I have to say, "in prayer!" No, my friend, I am not pushing for a cheap angelic stand. But confronted with such catastrophes, I simply need to believe that somewhere there is . . . God's grace.

And you, the atheist, do you have another solution, another

way to reach the capacity to accept our lot, our so often inhuman condition?

I so desire to talk about all this with you! Please, be not so seldom seen . . . I will be at La Madeleine until 5PM next Tuesday . . .

> *Your very sad and perplexed friend,*
> CLOTILDE

&

My dear Eugénie,

We are all so happy to learn that the birth of your little Paul went well and that you are both in excellent health. What joy for you and all your family. And it is a boy! You have really done things right!

I want to thank you also for having sent the lovely birth announcement. Receive all my best compliments! Mother is very impressed by the chic little card, and also by your audacity! Well, to present your newborn by his first name before his baptism is a sure sign of your "modernity!" Mother would say it is more your independence from the church. We will carefully safeguard the announcement, since it is the first we have ever received! A photograph will, perhaps soon, keep it company, since Pierre and you are so open to today's novelties!

That you would like to make me the godmother of your little Paul André is a great honor, but I understand fully Pierre's arguments: family first, and also, of course, someone having the means, from all points of view, to help this child during his life. Well, being single, living quite far from you, and having limited resources, how could I play such a role that today is still so essential in the life of a godson? Nor do I have any good contacts in either administration or industry that might help him succeed. I am certain that the godfather that Pierre is proposing possesses everything required. Moreover, his wife will certainly be a good godmother who can guide him, protect him, even spoil him, especially if he has the charms of his "big" sister, which I do not doubt for a minute! Rest assured, my friend, your Pierre is making the right choice!

Let me talk about Simone: how does she see this little being who now plays such a big part in your lives? Does she show surprise, curiosity, a little jealousy? Oh, I am so impatient to see you all and to cuddle your dear children!

Tell me soon the date of the baptism, and if a little visit beforehand might be possible.

> *Again, all my compliments and my most*
> *affectionate thoughts,*
> YOUR CLO WHO SENDS BIG HUGS TO YOU ALL

⚮

MONDAY, OCTOBER 4, 1897

My dearest Friend,

Your pretty card arrived just in time to remind me that Friday the first had a certain importance, and that attaining the age of 25 is a noteworthy event. Still, what is most touching is that in spite of your many concerns, the constant needs of your two little ones, your too-long days and too-short nights, you did not forget my birthday! Eugénie, you took the time to buy a pretty card; you found, like always, the perfect words that told me, as clearly as possible, the depth of the friendship that has bound us together these fifteen years! What happiness you bring me! Thank you, thank you! I can think of no greater pleasure, if not having you by my side, but that must wait another short month.

87

I must tell you also, as you thought, that I spent a lovely Friday evening. Indeed, Mother had invited, without telling me, my cousins Jules and Paul d'Argis, a nice surprise, and of course excellent conversation around a very well stocked table. Jean-Louis was not outdone since he had insisted on celebrating my birthday on Saturday at the Grand Vatel, just the two of us. A particularly enjoyable evening for us both.

But let us get back to your card and its news: I am so happy to know that your little Paul seems at ease in his new world since he hardly ever cries. Being able to enjoy those less-interrupted nights and those moments of rest mid-day is not due to chance, but to the fact that your little one can feel, with nary a doubt, the love, the constant attention you give him. And it is a just return, for the remarkable mother that you are!

Let me add that you are an equally remarkable wife: Pierre never stops telling me how happy he is to have you at his side, how lucky he is . . .

I am going to stop my compliments now, so that you will not be tempted to doubt them!

> *I send big hugs and include all my wishes that*
> *your life may continue this wonderful odyssey.*
> YOUR CLO

My very dear Eugénie,

What a pleasure to know that your little Simone loved the doll that I sent for her birthday! Four years old already, how time flies! I am also thrilled to know that she likes to sit at your piano and tries to imitate your vocal exercises. It must be a true joy for you! And her little brother? Will he be fascinated,

like his father, by automobiles? We will find out if we are right
in a couple of years . . .

Meanwhile, little news to share, for I am not going to talk
long about the Treaty of Paris, which you must have read
about in your local paper. I will simply say that, being more
on the side of the Cuban revolutionaries, I am quite happy
that Spain has abandoned the fight and that peace has
returned. Still, according to my cousin Auguste Guyot (who
is passionate about politics and plans a future in diplomacy)
there is naught to rejoice about yet, as the vast majority of
Cubans, who up till now have not had enough food to eat, will
not really benefit from this independence. In fact, according
to Auguste, American financial interests are opposed to a true
independence of this little country, whose economy relies on
the marketing of sugar cane.

I do not understand very well the relationship between
sugar and the right to justice and to a decent life for a
population that has for so long been "on a leash." But let us
leave that question for our diplomats and politicians to ponder
and get back to the news that affects us.

I completely share your reticence concerning a possible
departure for Sénégal, for we would be so far apart from each
other. But it would, in fact, be so useful for Pierre's career,
and he seems so interested in the development of colonial
administration. I have also heard that Saint-Louis is a very
agreeable city. Think, too, about all that you would discover in
that far away land. Your curiosity, your innate interest would
compensate for your regrets of being so far away from us. And
I know that you would write me long letters to share all of
your extraordinary discoveries! Yes, a two-year stay would be
a godsend for you as well as for Pierre. And too bad for this
Clotilde who would miss you so much. Oh, Eugénie, it is not

always easy to see the good side of things and to accept the "little" inconveniences, as Mother would say, but what other choice do we have? I simply believe that we have to concentrate on what we like, what reassures us.

So I have two pieces of good news to share with you: Jean-Louis is the most accommodating and attentive to my wants. Thus we will go to Pas-de-Calais to celebrate the New Year and will be able to stop in Arras along the way! The second is the news that, once again, three of my drawings have been accepted by Furnion company: my colors and patterns lending themselves well, apparently, to silk mapping. I could not ask for more!

I will stop here so that my letter may leave this evening, as I know you are impatient to hear from me.

> *Your friend who sends big hugs,*
> CLO

⌘

FRIDAY, 28 APRIL 1899

My dear Friend, (Jean-Louis Leroy)

Allow me to contradict you: the love that you have for me is a deep feeling no doubt, but it is not a passion. No, your passion lies elsewhere. It has occupied you for 15 years, day and night. It draws your attention to itself ceaselessly. This passion lives in you surely more than any passion for a woman, even though you are not devoid of feelings. You know how to love, you know how to take interest in those around you, but this jealous passion has you on such a short lease that a mere nothing takes you back to it. A noise in the street, a form, a color, everything brings it surging up, against your will. That is precisely why it is truly your passion.

I am not jealous of it, even though sometimes I wish it left me a little more place in your life. I cannot in fact imagine you without it, as if I were afraid to find you to be nothing but an empty shell. Am I rambling? Yes, perhaps a little, but I also know that there is no great inventor, no great thinker or artist who is not, like you, totally immersed in his passion. It does not change anything that with you, it is the automobile.

To prove to you that I am not mad at you or it, and, since you proposed it to me in such a charming fashion, I agree to take part in your exhibition at the fair next month. I will be there for the opening and the first three days, but afterwards, you will have to be content with brief appearances for I cannot abandon my work for Furnion Company: you know very well that in July we devote ourselves to the fabrics that will go on sale next winter.

That said, I admit I am a bit surprised: I who know so little about your machine, how can I be expected to promote it? You say all I need to do is present it. I imagine standing alongside it, caressing it with my hand, like a thoroughbred, opening the door and sitting in it as nonchalantly as possible, caressing its steering wheel so nicely covered in leather, smiling in a dreamlike manner, as if this machine should take me directly to paradise. I promise I will present my best profile to the photographers and will wear the enchanting hat that you gave me for the arrival of spring. But do you really believe, as you said to me with that smile that I cannot resist, that my simple presence would make your little car the star of the show? That asks a lot of my charm and shows little belief in your remarkable engineering gift!

Moreover I hope that you will not expect me to get a Certificate of Capacity[8] for, although I appreciate being driven about from time to time, I am not ready to become an "automobile chauffeur" and to run the risk of being the object of one of Charlus' songs.[9] I realize that you like above all its "humor" (as the English say), but what really bothers me in this song is its vulgarity. Am I really too severe in my judgment or have I learned the rules of decorum too well? I appeal to your clemency: do not make me drive your little car and do not sing that horrid song, at least not in public.

The tragic comedy of Georges Maurevert, *La Dernière soirée de Brummell,* will open on May 4TH at the Nouveau Theatre; do you want to go with us? We, Louise and I, think it is important to show our support for this die hard Dreyfusard.

Your too devoted Clo

SATURDAY, OCTOBER 14, 1899

Dear cousins,

Our discussion yesterday has started me thinking, so I am writing to better explain my position and that of Mother and Edouard in this "affair." I have a few arguments that should explain some of the differences in the midst of our family, like in all French families, apparently. But first let me tell you that, in spite of Auguste's mocking wit, I know well that you will share my point of view.

So, one cannot deny that the majority of newspapers have been particularly hard on the Dreyfusards and iniquitous to Zola! Now that he has returned from England, they have not hesitated to trot out the accusations against Zola the elder, among others! All this mud-slinging makes me sick because it is trying to hide an injustice with even more injustice! But let us continue. You, like me, have read Zola's article and have a bit known the Dreyfus family. Then, how can one believe the army's accusations against him? How can one take the side of the "liars?" Of course, we have to take into account our way of thinking, which is formed thanks to the models and principles inculcated in us since our youngest days. That explains our present difficulty in sorting out sometimes the why of our positions, and, of course, our divergence. So, be not surprised by Mother's silence; she received her convictions both from the lessons learned from the Sisters of Ferté-Gaucher (who certainly shared the traditional antisemitism of the catholic church and preached an absolute obedience to authority) as well as from Grandfather Guyot. Indeed, our civil servant never made many waves, but as a Free Mason, as you know, he had a most open mind, to the point of rebellion. He suffered too many iniquities from the ministries to take their side without question. Influenced by these two tendencies, Mother is, at the same time, little inclined to accuse the military hierarchy, while still unable to accept the condemnation of Dreyfus. Thus she listens to our arguments without really daring to take sides.

Edouard has similar tendencies but for different reasons. He was deeply influenced by Grandfather Théophile. You see, the Loevens have always maintained a sort of emigrant mentality. Although they came to France before the Revolution, they have never really taken part in the social movements that have so fired up the Faubourg for generations! No Jean-Louis, Eugène or Théophile on the barricades of 1830 or 1848, no Jean-Baptiste in the ranks of the Commune: worried about their status, they chose to remain in the shadows to observe events or to melt into the crowd even if it was hard for them to give in. With a Germanic sounding name, although in fact Jewish-Dutch, the men all, as you well know, married practicing Catholics, baptized their children and sent them to catholic schools. Even though their deepest convictions were close to those of Voltaire, Saint-Simon and other thinkers. According to

Mother, Grandfather Théo often said, during the Commune, "Let us do what is expected and keep our thoughts to ourselves." In that way, he was so like our Grandfather Guyot that it is not surprising that they were such good friends! As a young man, my father was less cautious, more deliberate in his words; he was more like the Amiard side of the family. We know from my Grandmother Marie-Elizabeth, that her brother did not hesitate to join the Commune (and came out the worse for it). Still, having come from the Loiret, and with a very French name, the Amiards cannot be accused of being Jewish spies working for Prussia! A Loeven, on the other hand, would have found it difficult to defend himself if he had found himself accused!

But to return to Edouard, it is clear that he, like all of you, knows quite well to what extent the members of the army and the police are exposed to the errors and injustices of their superiors. He told me that he is not the only one at the police station to question the motives of the Army and that the spirit of revenge leads to many excesses. He is careful not to take a very clear stand, but I know that his heart leans left, nearer to those whom he directs and oversees!

As for me, it is simple: if one has any heart, one should be on the side of the weakest, and if one has any common sense, one listen to those who, like Zola, have examined the affair before defending the one who is the victim of unjustified accusations, that are based particularly on a dreadful, indefensible antisemitism (undoubtedly due in part to the Panama scandal). It is so easy for officers to accuse their subordinates of treason in order to clear their own names! What a shame for France, what a sorrow for the innocent! Deep down, I understand the diatribes of Jules Vallès against the right, or the impassioned words of Louise Michel, even if I do not always share their energetic spirit . . .

So there you have, my dears, what I wanted to tell you a little more clearly, so that you may understand that our positions do not really clash. And who knows? Perhaps my arguments will bring you even closer to the good side: am I naive?

> *I impatiently await to see you all next Friday,*
> CLO

‹›

My dear Lov . . . (finish it as you please)

I came home this evening so disturbed by your words that I am unable to fall asleep. What in our discussion was so surprising, so troubling as to destabilize me thus? In the peace of my bedroom, I shall attempt to see more clearly and to share with you the thoughts that preoccupy me.

In the first place, I will say again: No, I am not your mistress, just as you are not my master. I am, simply, utterly your lover, just as you are my lover. It is a situation without ambiguity. Love is the sole reason for our relationship. And I believe that you love me as I love you. Your generosity, your concern for me, your constant support are the manifest proofs of your sentiment. I know that you recognize mine as identical to yours. Yes! We may also congratulate ourselves for not attempting to control the life of each other, even if sometimes we (read I) would like to occupy a more visible place in the life of the other . . . Am I right so far? Thus we are LOVERS. Yes! It is a good and fair proposition; a relation that suits me, a happiness that enthralls me.

So, you may ask, what is the source of your problem, of your insomnia? It is the word "mistress" that disturbs, infuriates me. And we both know that its meaning denotes a certain disdain for women, as there is no corresponding masculine form. After all, how are these women no one marries the mistresses of anyone at all? How do they ever make important decisions for you, sir? How do they govern your actions? How do they obtain your obedience? The master, on the other hand, holds our lives in his hands: every choice, every activity, every sentiment even, depends on his good will.

There are, of course, the school-mistress and the mistress of the household, but there the equation ends. Our great language does not propose dance mistress, mistress at arms, or mistress and commander, and even less mistress of the works or of the worksite. Where are the mistresses of thought, conference mistresses, choir mistresses? Finally, where are, among the artists, the Old Mistresses — despite the fact that there is no lack of women artists, even if they are yet not common enough?

Obviously there are some Masterly Women, but they are avoided whenever possible, and are rarely taken as one's mistress, of course.

Telling you all this comforts me. I see better what is actually at the heart of the subject. The status of women has to change. And I believe it will happen only when we improve the education of girls. The doors of the high schools and the universities must be open wide so women may finally enter these careers. As they find their role in those places, so far, forbidden, we will share a more equitable vocabulary. Then, and only then, will these expressions lose their degrading connotation for us, the women and girls, whom you claim to love so much!

I hear you laughing deep in your throat; better yet if my ideas amuse you. They are hardly new, nor are they proposed by a fool! You, who are somewhat literate, in spite of your passion for automobiles, must admit that Christine de Pisan and Madame de Scudéry spoke very well of women, and Olympe de Gouges and Pauline Léon demonstrated great courage, that

Flora Tristan and our Louise Michel are names that inspire young girls thirsty for Liberty, Equality and Fraternity (please, note the upper case).

But it is not a matter of touting "feminism" as Charles Fourier called it, or was it Hubertine Auclert . . . No, no need to burst out laughing, I do not read *La Fronde*, despite the fact that Marguerite Durand has excellent things to say about equality for women according to my cousin Jules (whose spirit you prize). You should know that he immerses himself in this publication religiously. Ah, yes, go figure why this confirmed bachelor who just celebrated his 38TH birthday yesterday reads this journal completely written and published by women! Perhaps, it is his way to better understand his brother Henri . . .

This evening has rather tired me, so I will end my letter here, but allow me simply to add that I love you just as you are, profoundly involved with your infernal machines. On this subject, bravo for the design of your latest creation: I see the touch of your designer on your sedan, this "interior driving" (as you so beautifully put it). You should be very proud, and reassured for the future of your enterprise!

I remain merely Your . . . Lover,

CLO

இ

THURSDAY, JANUARY 9, 1902

My dear Eugénie,

I hope that you arrived at the Gare de l'Est yesterday in time to welcome your visitors. I impatiently wait for you to tell me in detail how you found your dear little cousin.

I promised to tell you everything about the continuation of our discussion with the Amiards, since they have managed to pique your curiosity. Please know that the conversation left behind the anecdotes on life in the Loiret, the beauty of the Briare canal bridge and Thomas' meeting with the great Gustave Eiffel, quickly took an unexpected as well as personal turn; they had the presumption to question my relationship with Jean-Louis because they deem it to be "unfortunate!" Thomas added that they both admire my talents and my humor, but that concerning my life as a woman, I lack discernment. Victorine even whispered that it would be better if I called it off right away for, and I quote: "a future as a 'grande horizontale' is not to be envied and would bring dishonor to the entire family!"

I was unable to speak for a minute. Then I asked them how they dared treat me like that since, far from being "kept," I work and contribute fully both toward the expenses of our household and to other needs of my mother. I even pointed out that my plebeian roots did not at all push me toward a life of frivolity, deceit, and scandal; that up till now I had been able to be discrete and trustworthy; that money did not compare to the happiness brought about by honest feelings and self respect. I added that I shared Victorine's feelings about the unenviable fate of kept women, who often let themselves be lured by bourgeois men imprisoned by their own vanity as much as by their libertinism. And to finish, I insisted that if my good cousins were finding it too difficult to be around me, given my attachment to a man "who is not good for me," I would understand if they no longer opened their door to me, at which, in any case, I would no longer be knocking. I turned around and left them in the middle of the street, as their jaws dropped! They must have arrived home thinking that I was decidedly unreasonable and quite impertinent. I wonder, moreover, if they had not been charged with "teaching me a lesson" and bringing me back to the "righteous path" by some other member of the family, but which one or ones?

What is almost amusing, is that our Amiards have not always observed the "morals" that they flaunt today! In fact, we all know that their eldest son, Eugène, kept his mother's name for four years, and that our Victorine was worried stiff when her mother-in-law presented the little boy to the family the day before her wedding with Thomas. As you know, the legitimacy of a child is not a pertinent question for me, especially if the mother finds a man happy to love the child. Having said that, I do not at all regret my anger and never seeing them again suits me fine. Edouard, who sees them but rarely anyway, assured me that "it will not be a great loss" when I told him about the incident. Of course I have not said a word about it to Mother, but I know that she has never felt close to them and does not insist on seeing them; after all, they are only the nephews of her mother-in-law. And although Mother enjoyed the kindness of grandmother Loeven, she rarely saw the Amiards much, even when they lived on Bercy Street. Family ties are thus undone . . .

And you, what do you think of all that? Do you share my indignation? Or was I perhaps too brutal? I must say that I surprised myself with the violence of my reaction, being usually calm and fairly accommodating (too much sometimes?). I think that I am in a period of doubt about my existence. My current unease is undoubtedly the cause of my behavior, for I must confess that I am at a time in my life where nothing is simple any more, nor as clear as even six months ago. It seems that everything has been said, and that according to my choice, never would I have a family of my own. That choice was made in view of my own family experience, reinforced by those of my mother and my grandmother: does not marriage end, almost always, by betrayal, abandonment, or widowhood? Should not we prefer a relationship that lasts but which can be dissolved if one of us sees the necessity? Is it not true that if I found myself alone tomorrow, I would be saddened by it, but not emptied of all my substance like so many others have been before and in front of me? Pain sharpens our feelings, despair destroys us. We must avoid the latter to the best we can. I have always thought that if J-L were to decide that marriage with another were required, I would bow to it without too much bitterness. After all, I was the one who refused marriage two years ago. He did not seem to suffer much from it, I must say! But, up till now our arrangement suits me/us just fine.

Still, since Christmas, a little doubt has appeared that hardly lets me rest. Of course, you are the first to have put me on my guard when I refused his proposal. Prudence would have had me leave him for good. But we have such a need to know we are admired, loved, respected. You have told me so yourself, many times. Your brief relationship with Jean Benoît being more stormy, it was easier for you to break it off and go on. But for me it was, it is the "ideal relationship," or almost. Up till now Jean-Louis has led his life like he always wanted to, faithful in his commitment but at the same time free of constraints. I am, he says, the love of his life. I supposedly bring him a necessary balance without infringing on his freedom which he cannot do without. That freedom, that independence, I also claim it, which was often a little difficult given his tendency to control everything, as you know. But this independence has suddenly lost a little of its appeal; and I do not really know why. What has changed so much in me, around me? Nothing that I can discern.

I do not want to abuse your patience, so I am going to stop here, but please know that I truly appreciate your insight, your incomparable intuition when it comes to delving into the human soul. Tell me what you think of all that. Should I break off with Jean-Louis, and marry some old man, or a widower a little less worn out? There are plenty backstage at the Vaudeville Theater or at the Ambiguous (we will never find a better word). I am making fun, a little, but my malaise is real. Come to my aid, my friend.

I will be rehearsing at Saint Eustache until 5 o'clock Friday, do you want to meet me there? We could go for tea at Stohrer, I know you adore their babas.

See you very soon, my Friend, my "Savior"
YOUR CLO

P.S.: Could you please reassure your little Simone for me? Tell her that I have not forgotten her request and will send the little silk scarf for her big doll before mid-Lent. Hug her for me, and also little Paul-André and his daddy.

૯౨

VIENNA, JUNE 30, 1902

My sweet Eugénie,

Keeping my promise, I am announcing the news that you can share with Monsieur Pierre without ado: WE WON! Marcel covered himself with glory in the little K6!!! Are you surprised? You are not alone: absolutely no one expected it!

Just imagine: 1,300 kilometers in under 30 hours on the road, or an average speed of 62.5 kilometers per hour. Imagine too, that he outdistanced 148 other competing vehicles including the Panhard and the Mercedes cars with large engines, which were favored! We cannot get over it! Louis is absolutely "enchanted." What an extraordinary success. You said to me two or three years ago: "This young man will go far." But would you have predicted that he would complete Paris to Vienna in under four days in this little car open to the wind and the road dust?

This grand exploit is explained by the lightness of the car on the mountain roads, which are merely, as we know only too well, curves adorned with ravines and clouds of blinding dust, since these roads are not paved. It is thus extremely difficult to pass others and maintain a speed greater than that of a horse! But here are a few details in a language that Monsieur Pierre will understand, no doubt: with its 4 cylinders in two blocks (?), its 3,770 cubic centimeters (?) its 1,100 rpms rolls (of what?) per minute, and 24 horsepower (I am speaking here like an expert, even though I have no idea what it all means, as my "?" indicate), the little K6 conquered all obstacles. This incredible victory is due to rapid acceleration on hills and an impressive road-holding according to Louis, who, on the other hand, did not have the control of his brother and broke a wheel trying to pass a competitor, between Bregenz and Salzburg. Despite all these lovely explanations, I most want to see in this success the mastery of Marcel, our great champion-driver-racer-pilot. He has really earned all those names!

And would you believe me if I told you that he is happy with his success but takes no pride in it? That is a distinguished man! All the ladies would obviously love his company. For my part, I would be more reserved: the life of an auto racing champion is not worth much. Who would want to live in fear day after day? Perhaps I have grown too timorous with age. In any case, waiting for the leading cars at the finish line in Vienna gave me a foretaste of what pilots' wives endure.

Marcel Renault at the wheel of his K6.

Nonetheless, our sojourn in Austria is wonderful. The atmosphere in Vienna is electric! We meet, all day long, remarkable people from the industrial world, mostly the automobile. Invitations rain down, wonderful dinners are the norm. I let myself be guided without resisting in the least in this constant effervescence, but I am not always very attentive to the conversation around me: the world of engineers and manufacturers — often the same people — is rather obscure for those of us who center on art and music. If your sweet husband wants more details about mechanical matters, procedures and other technical subjects, he will need to speak directly to the engineers responsible for that prowess.

They are already making plans for a race from Paris to Madrid next summer. Nothing stops progress or the ambition of the young men of our era, as you well know!

There you are, my Dear, the news that the papers in your far away province will surely bring you. Édouard has promised — and you know we can count on him to hold his promises — to buy and save the *Petit Journal Illustré* for those who want more details about this event, considered to be a national victory! In that regard, when will you be returning to Paris? Your parents tell me you plan to move to Lille next winter. Does Paris really hold no attraction for you, for both of you? Write to me, at rue de la Forge Royale, if you are unable to come for a visit. In the meantime, I will keep you posted on the latest gossip of the rue du Ranelagh.[10]

> *Yours affectionately,*
> CLOTILDE

My very dear Eugénie,

Thank you so much for your charming letter and the reassuring news. But your absence yesterday evening was felt: we all missed your scintillating repartee. That said, who would have thought that such a cumbersome birthday could be so joyous? It must be said that I share it with the great Sarah Bernhardt, who managed to reach 58 years, if I can believe my indiscreet sources. So how could I feel sad about my plight? Admit it, I have more to celebrate than poor Julie d'Aiglemont,[11] whom we are forced to pity, since Balzac feels sorry for her. No, the woman of thirty that I am does not see the end of her thirst, far from it!

So, let me tell you quickly how we celebrated this happy event, with the three inseparable Renault brothers, Jeanne, Suzanne and me, no more, no less — J-L. is in London until the 9TH. Early in the evening we enjoyed Marcel Schwob's play, *Francesca da Rimini,* a gripping spectacle at the Sarah Bernhardt Theater, and then a wonderful dinner at the Zimmer Restaurant across the street. This was an evening designed to delight even the saddest of thirty-year-old women.

The choice of this play is not without interest, for it confronted us with a truth: the jealousy of some always causes the unhappiness of others. As you may remember the passage in the *Divine Comedy* (on which Marcel Schwob's play is based), where Francesca da Rimini, married to a man she does not love, falls for her young brother-in-law, the seductive Paolo. The husband surprises them exchanging a kiss, and, mad with jealousy, kills them both with one stroke of his sword. One cannot imagine a play more romantic and edifying!

The conversation at the table of course was centered on marriages (arranged or not), impossible love and misguided jealousy. We were all happy to have avoided, until now, this catastrophic destiny. Then, our laughters were interrupted by the waiter who was bringing our cake — a delicious one!

But let us return to the play. Our glorious actress Sarah Bernhardt played (on her own stage, mind you!) the role of Francesca de Rimini in this piece, which she had requested of Francis Crawford, no doubt to match that of Stephen Phillips, which was such a success last spring in London, as you know. However, despite the magnificent sets, and a staging, which reached the heights of all expectations, the play did not evoke in me the same emotion as the poetic symphony of Tchaikovsky. Perhaps our Lady Bernhardt is a bit too old for this role of a young lover at the hands of a cruel destiny.

Not everyone agreed with me, but it was mostly to deny me the last word; you know how Fernand loves to impose his views on people —particularly on Jeanne (who would never contradict her husband.) Nonetheless the evening went very nicely in the warm atmosphere of the Zimmer. What an agreeable place with its setting so well adapted to today's taste! It is also exciting to meet many celebrities within its walls: Camille Pissarro was leaving as we entered. Yes! We must go there when you come to Paris. But rest assured, you will not be forced to eat a dish of sauerkraut, even if the owners (Alsatians, of course) claim it is the best in Paris. For my part, I preferred a delicious slice of roast veal. Their sundaes, by the way, have no equal, and I am not even talking about their famous *apfeltorte*. It is definitely a wonderful place to go and share a meal with friends; I am sure that Pierre and you would truly appreciate it as much as I do.

I should not forget to mention the nice gift the Renault brothers gave me: a very pretty case with two cigarette holders, one short and one long, of ivory; a perfect marvel which, Louis says, will be the most sought after object in two or three years (they want me at the forefront of fashion!).

In fact, I do not smoke much, and only in their company. I do not have to tell you that Mother does not suffer smoke and prefers not to know that her precious daughter lights a cigarette now and then . . . She also avoids any mention of J-L for she still has a hard time accepting our "situation," in spite of the many discussions we had about my stand on marriage. Yes, silence rather than truth! Will we be like her when we get to be her age?

My dear Eugénie, tell me in detail about the progress of Pierre in his new position as inspector in the Commissioner's office, the frolics of your adorable children, as well as your new "occupation" at the cathedral. Your voice will be marvelous there! But I must leave you now since I am reaching the end of my candle and need to work a bit more on my drawings before I find the soothing sleep my numerous years demand. Do not laugh, you who are younger — even if only by eight months!

I await your return with great impatience!

> *With tenderness*
> YOUR CLO

℀

PARIS, NOVEMBER 13, 1902

My dear Friend,

Your letter got to me a little late; might the postmen have lost some of their efficiency in light of the cold and somber weather? But that does not stop me from truly appreciating your questions. Actually, Eugénie, your well-placed curiosity warms my heart and shows me that you really care about my happiness. So it is with pleasure that I am going to answer. But before that, I want to remind you again that concerning my relationship with Jean-Louis, you are the only person with whom I can share my thoughts. And never mind if most of the questions we ask ourselves remain unanswered.

So for your question about the true nature of our relationship. To tell the truth, I am not sure I can precisely describe it. I believe that our shared attachment is based now on a deep friendship, one of the strongest feelings. And that is because over the last few months our physical passion has slowly changed: it has lost its importance. And I do not really know if my refusal to marry him is the cause or the consequence of this change. I lean a little more toward the cause. Still, I am happy with my decision because, as I told you, there were too many things that I could not accept: his fortune, his passion for his machines, his inability to go outside his own world, his appetite for women. All of that, little by little, nibbled away at our relationship. But a real affection binds us together and I feel it will last.

Did I ever hope to marry him? Frankly? No! You know that I do not trust marriage. And I have never met a man who could put me completely at ease; a man in whom I could have absolute confidence. I do not even know if such a man exists, except for your noble husband, of course!

You will say that I am depriving myself of the happiness of having children And I understand you, given my attachment to your Simone and Paul André. They are both charming and irresistible! You know how I love to spend hours with them, how I spoil them (too much perhaps), but I cannot think about having my own children That side of a woman's life is too bound to the existence of the couple. Being single and having decided to remain so, I do not see myself in the sad role of unmarried mother. A child born of an "unknown" father is out of place in our middle class, patriarchal world, and I would be unable to deprive a child of the love and support of its father. Thus the affection of my godchildren will suffice.

Growing old alone? That will, therefore, be my fate, unless

Edouard decides to marry. That would allow me perhaps to
have nieces and nephews inclined to take care of their aunt.
That is actually a highly unlikely possibility, as he also, till now,
has been careful not to wed, or to find a sister soul (not me,
his sister, clearly; what an interesting expression!).

Such are my succinct answers to your questions. Does that
help you better see where I am? Is your experience as a (so
well-) married woman going to help you light my way? Do you
really think that a better understanding of the facts and of our
urges can change the course of things if not of our future? It
is possible that thanks to a certain "wisdom" we make more
"reasonable" choices. But, actually, better understanding all that
lets us accept that future, live fully, without too many regrets,
and at the end, find peace.

After all this "philosophizing" I leave you to your many
duties and wish you a week full of joy and happiness with your
dear family.

YOUR CLOTILDE

࿐

PARIS, MAY 24, 1903

My dear Friends,

Thank you so much for your thoughts and condolences.
Yes, we are devastated by Marcel's passing, and still surprised,
even though that accident, that brutal death was predictable:
I used to think about it incessantly. But the pleasure, the
excitement that automobile racing (or any other) causes are
too strong to slow down the hero, the next winner. Pierre, you
are in a better position to understand those feelings that leave
us bewildered, we women who are too easily frightened, too
sentimental, perhaps.

Yes, I have lost a great friend, but how could I possibly

understand the despair of Marthe Renault? Marcel was her favorite son in many respects. Fernand is just as shocked and his health is suffering from it. We are all of us plunged into a deep mourning . . .

I must add that there were four other racers and three spectators who met death during that crazy race. One speaks little of them, but those beings also deserve our thoughts and regrets.

Thank god, the only woman, Camille de Gast, who was in the race got out safe and sound, but she is far from having won.

Louis, in spite of his great victory, sees this tragedy as a sign of destiny. He now wants to concentrate his energy on the manufacture of his cars and their brake systems in particular, and not on racing, not on competition. That will be passed on to the young "professionals" who are thinking only about the challenge.

And that, my friends, is all I can tell you for the time being. In a few months we will see more clearly, I hope! But for that our sadness is not any less deep. So take good care of yourselves and your little ones. Be careful, as much as possible!

> *I send big hugs,*
> Your very sad Clotilde

P.S.: Yes, Eugénie, you are right, the accident happened in the Poitou region, at Couché-Vérac, the village that was more or less the end of the first quarter of the Paris-Madrid course.

~

PARIS, JULY12, 1903

My very dear Eugénie,

Your letter, so full of enchanting details concerning your adorable children, arrived just in time to give me some courage of which I am sorely in need.

Well, it is all over: Jean-Louis and I separated with nary a tear. Do not worry, we are still friends! That is, I can count on him should I be in such need, and he can meet me according to his mood. I appreciate his friendship that will certainly remain faithful, but I really do not know exactly where I stand. And yet, I was expecting this since, for several months now, our relationship had stretched thin; we no longer shared those sweet moments, those intoxicating evenings, those thrilling discussions. Our paths were more and more divergent.

The why of this change in our relationship, for me, is now quite clear: after the deaths of his father and his brother, a great need to rebuild a family took hold of him. He wants to find a woman who will agree to marry him, to give him children. He may even have someone in mind, but that is not the question. As for me, I turned down his proposal; I was unable to take that leap, to give him what he needs so badly.

As you know, I cannot help but think of marriage as a vise, a stranglehold. And yet all around me I have examples of happy unions: yours in particular! Have I lost my mind? It is not impossible, but what good does it do to question myself? I have to go forward. That will not be too difficult, for I will find, without a doubt, an appeasing balm with my family and friends — of which you are the flag-bearer!

You see, just writing all of this to you already gives me a certain self-confidence and a little of the enthusiasm that you will appreciate, as always.

I will write again soon. Meanwhile, keep me apprised of the progress that Paul André is making in reading. I have several little books to give him.

I send hugs and kisses to the four of you,
CLO

SATURDAY, JANUARY 3, 1905

My dear Auguste,

Mother, Edouard and I hope you are still in good health and happy to be in the beautiful city of London. We did indeed receive your best wishes for the end of the year in response to ours. May God grant them all!

And one of our wishes has just been granted, since we move tomorrow: Edouard has, in fact, found the most practical lodgings for us on Crozatier Street, at the corner of Citeaux Street, which you know well.

We are leaving Royal Forge Street with no regrets, in spite of our habits; we were feeling more and more cramped. This time, each of us will have his own bedroom. It is an apartment on the fifth floor, looking out over the street and with a pretty view of the Eiffel Tower, in a brand new apartment building. What a difference compared to the one we are leaving! Henceforth we will have, apart from three bedrooms, a pretty dining room with balcony, a small kitchen with a little window over the courtyard, and a bathroom. The water closet is on the landing, just across from our front door. In short, an apartment where it will be nice to welcome you. I must add that the pieces of furniture signed 'Loeven' are looking young again: Mother has been busy cleaning and vigorously waxing them, which she had not done for several months.

I believe that this change will do her a lot of good. The Faubourg weighs heavily on her. We will not be far away, so she will be able to keep her most faithful clients, but at the same time she will not be confronted day after day by those places that first knew her so happy, then so bitter, and that for more than twenty years.

The nearness of the Aligre market and of Boulevard Diderot is not displeasing either. Also, St. Eloi Church, which you must know, is modern, light, and much more welcoming than Sainte Marguerite, too full of mournings for us. We could not ask for more in this move! We await visits and mail at this address: 46 rue Crozatier, Paris 12ᵉ arrondissement.

But let us talk a little about you: do you plan to stay in London, or are you going to opt for Buenos Aires? And what about Canada? Your path intrigues me: can one really make a fortune selling old furniture? According to your parents it would seem so since, apart from being a talented artist, you also have a sense for business: bravo! I much admire your love for traveling, your ability to adapt; and your business success reminds us that you are truly a Guyot! I would not say as much for Edouard, who claims to be quite comfortable in his role as "police officer" and to not miss woodworking. I am not sure I believe him, but I also have abandoned my idea of becoming a renowned harpist, and content myself with a few little concerts here and there, and sometimes, even, at Saint Eustache church.

The time to post my mail approaches so I will stop here. But you must know that we await news from you with impatience and that we send affectionate hugs.

CLOTHILDE

Clotilde Loeven,
1912 & 1932

Chapter III
Another Self

Letters from March 1910 to January 1942 sent to

Eugénie

Auguste Guyot

Alexandre and Rose Guyot

Angèle, her sister-in-law

Jacqueline, her niece

Louis Renault, an old friend

❧

Maria Loeven enjoying the view from the balcony of their new apartment, on the sixth floor, 1913.

My dear Auguste,

I hope the post-office will be able to forward my letter to Bordeaux without too many difficulties, now that the flood in Paris has dissipated. I just simply want to reassure you. Edouard has overcome this catastrophic situation by giving so much of himself: many nights with no sleep, and an insurmountable frustration when he came to realize that he could hardly help all those people who, having lost everything, were in the greatest distress.

Paris flood, 1910

The damage to ground floors is in fact unimaginable, that is, not only in apartments, but also and especially in workshops, stores, factories, and small neighborhood businesses, without mentioning cellars: all their contents have been completely destroyed.

Crozatier Street was not spared, given the proximity of the Seine and of the Arsenal Canal. In fact, our little grocer and the bookseller who is next door to him have lost everything. Talking to them would break your heart! You can thus imagine how happy we are to live on the sixth floor!

Add to all that the mountains of detritus that clutter the streets and gardens. I do not see how our city will regain its equilibrium, or the Parisians their smile!

On the other hand, we can finally drink our water without worrying too much. But we remain vigilant.

Here is a nicer bit of news: Edouard has received a substantial pay raise of 100 francs that will greatly compensate for Mother's losses since her clients have almost all been affected by the flood. What is more, her tools and fabrics have not been ruined, as were those of so many other seamstresses!

As for me, do not worry: I am still working for the silk manufacturer in Lyon and for Blanchet Company, which, far from the Seine and its tributaries, had no damage at all, and will undoubtedly benefit from the current undoing of many of its competitors.

I leave you now, hoping to receive good news from you soon.

> *Kisses from*
> CLO

೮

My dear Auguste,

I hope you are in better health and will soon be able to begin your trip to the Antilles, as planned. I would so like to be part of that adventure!

Knowing how much our Candide Couzin liked Gaudeloupe's warm welcome, I wonder if it is not his infatuation that leads you to those sunny horizons. In fact, I believe more and more, upon aging, that we are all profoundly marked by those who surround us, even if we claim an independent spirit! Thus we arrive at the same conclusions, at the same choices. It is time to recognize the limits of our reasoning and the weight of our unconscious as Karl von Hartmann has shown so aptly — I expect a little note of admiration from you concerning the breadth of my knowledge . . .

But I am not writing to engage you in a philosophical discussion, but to announce with great pleasure that I have found new lodgings: a beautiful two-rooms on the ground floor in a brand new apartment building at 73 Bois-Bonnet Street, in Maisons-Lafitte. And yes, I will soon (in three short days) be settled in this fairly sophisticated suburb of our capital. Of course, it is thanks to our good friend Alfred de Berlantier that I owe this opportunity (he knows the owner).

My departure from Crozatier Street is not due to some long-repressed desire on my part for "independence." In fact, it turns out that Mother has more and more difficulty climbing our six floors. So Edouard is looking for an apartment on the ground floor in the Aligre neighborhood, not too far from his police station. Even though we know that ground floors rarely have more than two bedrooms. Now you know why I am leaving the family cocoon without too much regret. What is more, I will be much closer to my employer who is in Argenteuil.

I must add that the beautiful, unexpected, summery weather will make my move easier, which will be simple enough given the few things in my possession.

Send us your news soon, else I will have to speak to your parents!

> *Your adorable cousin who sends big hugs,*
> CLOTILDE

MONDAY, MARCH 30, 1914

My dear Auguste,

Thank you so much for your letter and your good news. We are happy that you met a young, oh-so-charming Parisian artist in London, and that you plan to take her to Montreal with you. It might be that she can help you widen the field of your business, given the prestige of French women in Canada, which is so attached to its roots. Send us more details about this young Marie, and on your commercial and other dealings, to satisfy our curiosity, since, like always, we want to be in the know!

Another piece of good news: your parents came by the house last Sunday, and we had a lovely time sharing memories along with a lot of nice food! Mother loves the wit of your father (her favorite cousin!), a wit that reminds her of her grandfather, "a true Guyot" as she says.

Finally, I must say that the move to Chaligny Street was a good idea: Mother and Edouard are quite happy there. I will add that the large windows that give on to the street and the courtyard ought to let in a lot of light, when the rain stops, which everyone is impatiently awaiting. In fact, we have rarely seen such a rainy March, but what can we do against the decisions of the heavens? Well, we can amuse ourselves; so I come to your question.

Yes, we did indeed celebrate Mid-Lent, which was an insane Thursday, in the great hall of the City Hall of the 12ème arrondissement. Dance was the main theme: not quadrilles, but polkas, mazurkas, waltzes, boleros, and of course tangos that would have thrilled you, you who feel Argentinian rhythms in every fiber of your being! That is not the case for me, but Edouard is closer to you in that realm.

Indeed, I can assure you that he had a field day, spending lots of time with Angèle, the young woman from Touraine who has worked at the Forestiers for several years. You may remember her: fairly tall, blond with blue eyes. She dances quite well, and seems to enjoy the witticisms of those around her; but I doubt that Edouard will make this Angèle a long-term companion: she is twenty years younger and does not appear to be very well educated. What will be will be! Meanwhile, their very frenzied waltzes got all the attention and applause in the room, to the great displeasure of the gentlemen, married or not, who were lacking female admirers. It was not therefore hard for me, at 42 years of age, to find rather charming dance partners who knew the mazurka. You know how I find that triple-time dance captivating thanks to the works of Chopin and Saint-Saëns that resonate in me as soon as the piano and accordion get a hold of it. That pleasure of the dance, however, has still not lead me to a man I might seduce. Too bad, next time maybe.

So there you have, for the time being, news from your cousins who think often of you and wish you a wonderful time in London. "See you soon."[12]

CLO

P.S.: You can tell that my English is always present, thanks to you!

෴

MAISONS, APRIL 20, 1914

My dear Eugénie,

What pleasure to have been able to spend those few days with you and your children! It was the very best Easter present that was ever given to me! There is no need to tell you again how glad I am about your return to Paris next winter.

Yes, our lives have really changed, but that has not lessened our friendship at all, in fact it has deepened. How lucky we are! What a godsend to be able to count on each other whatever our needs or circumstances! You cannot imagine how grateful I am to you!

But let us not spend too much time on ourselves, and let us come to the news that you are asking about. Edouard's newest little love will certainly not last longer than the earlier ones, even though this Angèle is young, steady and devout. One might be tempted to believe that, at 48 years of age, my brother could try to "tie the knot;" but I doubt it for he shares the reserve I have about marriage. Moreover, Mother does not see this relationship favorably, because her son is the man upon whom her life depends. She cannot imagine him leaving her; no woman can take him from her. Besides, I do not know if he would do so unless he were madly in love, which apparently is not the case, once again.

I must add that my brother shares hardly anything about his love life with me, since forever, whereas I never hesitated to talk to him about mine, nor to ask him his opinion although he hardly seemed to understand my enthusiasms, my needs for love. We even had some spirited arguments concerning my liaison with Jean-Louis, over the years. I think he considers me a hard-headed child who thought she was allowed anything! I do not know what he thinks now about my life as a solitary woman . . .

To come back to Edouard's relationship with this young woman, I would simply say that it is still too early to have a clear idea about it. When things move forward, I will hasten to satisfy your concern (the word "curiosity" not being appropriate in our milieu).

Meanwhile, we are going to enjoy an agreeable spring and think about your coming to Paris in June. I will welcome you to Maisons-Lafitte with the greatest pleasure!

> *I send big hugs to all five of you,*
> YOUR OLD CLOTILDE

❦

MAISONS-LAFITTE, THURSDAY, AUGUST 13, 1914

My very dear Friend,

I am glad to hear that you are all in Limoges, far from these terrible happenings, and especially happy that your son is not yet old enough to be called up. My young cousin, Jean-Paul Boucher d'Argis, and so many others are not so lucky and are heading for the front. May God hear our prayers and protect them.

We took the reassuring decision to bring Mother to my house in Maisons-Lafitte where she will be less exposed to enemy attacks; just as your parents had the good idea to join you in Limoges for the duration of the conflict, which we hope will be very short.

Still, we, like so many others, are terribly anxious. Mother, who knew the horrors of the last war, is terrified. She suffered so much during the siege and the famine that followed, which lasted more than four months! Today, according to Edouard, we must expect intense bombardments on the capital and its surroundings given the developments made in heavy artillery, and especially the Prussian long-range cannons. Needless to say, Mother and I are very worried about Edouard, as well as our cousins and friends who are still in our city. But what can we do?

The newspapers deny the possibility of Paris being invaded and occupied, but it is hard for me to keep such hope in the face of a Prussian army that is so powerful, so well-prepared.

Oh, my Eugénie, those events are so frightening that I can think of nothing else. I am going to close and mail this letter, as quickly as possible so that it may reassure you about us. Let us hope that the postal service is not interrupted and that I can have news from you soon.

Please, give my best wishes to your parents.

> *With all my affection and my prayers that you*
> *may all remain safe and sound!*

Your Clotilde

༄

MONDAY, OCTOBER 26, 1914

My dear Auguste,

Thank you for your short letter telling us about your return from Montreal, and your new address in London. So it is up to me, being in Paris today, to answer you.

First of all, we are happy to hear that your health is better and that the new treatment seems more efficient than the earlier ones. Still, you must consider the gravity of that persistent fistula as a blessing, since it has perhaps saved your life! Indeed, when you consider the massacres of the last three months, it is clear that being discharged is a great privilege, whatever the reason. In fact, it has become the dream of many young men who, until now, considered themselves true patriots. I am sure that your parents are happy, as are we, about your departure for England, neither one being particularly "vengeful," even though they experienced the horrors of the siege of 1870.

As you might imagine, news from the front is unceasingly

worrisome. Reconnaissance planes fly over Paris; entire regi-
ments pass through our train stations; everyone worries about
provisions for our troops; we are not given any numbers on
our losses, but calling up the reserves says a lot. I, for one, am
quite afraid that the massacres have only just begun. Neither
Edouard nor I think it will be a quick war; the Germans are
too well-prepared to be defeated as easily as our leaders would
have us believe. Of course the departure of the government for
Bordeaux and the declaration of Paris as a fortified town under
martial law do nothing to reassure us. Mother can no longer
cope: she imagines that the enemy will chase down our leaders
clear to Bordeaux, leaving only ruins in their wake. And I have
to admit that her fear is growing on us since the Germans
occupied Senlis, and that in less than a month! Our troops'
efforts to push them back to the Marne did not stop them
from seizing Reims in spite of the Paris taxis taking the troops
to the front! You probably know how the fire in the cathedral
on September 19 outraged the French people and, I think
even, a few Germans . . . After all, it was the Kaiser's wounded
soldiers who then occupied the cathedral, transformed into a
field hospital!

Due to a lack of buses and trucks, the French army officially requested all the taxis in Paris to transport the soldiers near the front, in September 1914, during the battle of the Marne, leaving few buses for civilians.

What terrifies us is the idea that air bombardments will surely take aim on Paris. Lunéville, which was bombed last week, is not so far, and our French aviators' response is only going to push Germany to intensify its attacks. We Parisians do not know which saints to pray to. Those who can are going to the countryside, but for most of us, flight is not even imaginable; we must hope that we will be spared the worst of it. Edouard, as a police officer and given his age, remains at his post, which is reassuring, especially for Mother who cannot imagine living without him.

But let us talk of less painful things: Edouard's little infatuation with Angèle Schmit has been over for a few months. He was not about to respond to the expectations of that rather nice young woman. I am not saying a word, as no one can tell a Loeven how to steer his boat . . .

And you? Where do you stand with Marie? You never told us how you met, nor why she was in London. But perhaps I should respect your discretion, which is, undoubtedly, legitimate or even necessary. So I will close this letter and hope that it will reach you soon, given that the mails are day by day more uncertain.

> *Your Clotilde, who awaits news from you*
> *with great impatience.*

ↄ৴ↄ

My dear Auguste,

Many thanks for your letter that we received on Monday, which reassured us about your life in London. We are thrilled to know that you are walking better after that painful bout with your kidneys: you must, as you say, be patient.

On this side of the Channel, nothing new: Mother's health continues to worsen, which is not surprising given her age and her persistent diabetes. Edouard is very busy at the police station, as you must imagine, as am I, given the considerable number of uniforms to deliver each week. Anyway, I am not going to talk to you about the battles that you must read about in the English papers, nor about the tramway strike, nor about the misery and fear that has been living in us for more than two long years. No, I am going to tell you something quite joyful that I just learned, and which is going to surprise you: Edouard met again Angèle Schmit! Yes! Marie and you have thus lost your bet and I await your return so that I may savor my victory in your company . . .

Here are some details that Edouard shared with me last night, well away from Mother's ears. Sunday, toward the end of the evening, my sweet brother found himself facing Angèle on the metro platform; it turns out that she has been the supervisor of the Reuilly station for several months. She seemed happy to see him, so he invited her for a coffee at 8:00 pm on Monday. That second meeting was rather pleasant, so they will see each other again next Sunday!

Edouard said nothing more, except that he was "fairly pleased" to renew contact with the young woman. And this is a good thing for, at 50 years of age, our Edouard really deserves a little comfort, pleasure, and why not, some passion in his life. I do not know what Mother will think if this relationship should end in marriage, but we are not there yet.

What do you think of that news? I eagerly await your response!

> *Big kisses for both of you,*
> YOUR OLD CLOTILDE

TUESDAY, JANUARY 20, 1917

My dear Auguste,

We received your letter of the 12TH, and are surprised, but happy, to learn of your return, safe and sound, from New York, while German submarines are dangerously prowling the waters of the Channel and the Atlantic. Of course London has not been sheltered from the attacks of the German Imperial Aircraft, according to the newspapers. Still, you are far from those trenches that are so deadly! But I cannot tell you anything new on this topic and that is not why I am writing. In fact, now that I know more, I simply want to satisfy your desire to learn about the "relationship between Edouard and his little minx" as you so nicely put it in your letter. So, I am going to share a secret that up till now has been well kept by my brother.

Since their chance encounter, Angèle had become more and more loquacious, which Edouard did not expect (after almost three years of silence!). Thus, she told him that she had been working in the metro for three months to provide for her family; that her brother had died in December of 1914 following wounds received in the trenches, in Ardennes; and that before getting the job in the metro, she had "looked after" newborns taken in by Saint Antoine church. Edouard complimented her on her courage, but was surprised that she had not returned to the Tours region where it must surely be easier to live in these times of war. Her answer was most surprising: she earned much more selling her milk in Paris than doing any other work in Noizay; and her mother took very good care of her little Jacqueline. Edouard, not daring to ask the obvious question, asked why she had stopped being a wet nurse. She smiled sadly and confessed that after several very serious asthma attacks, she had lost her ability to make milk, six months ago now. She had then been employed by an elderly couple who lived in her building on Saint Antoine Street, before obtaining her position in the CMP.[13]

I think you have already guessed what he learned next . . . Indeed, it turns out that little Jacqueline is his daughter, too!

Edouard told me that Angèle's revelation had not really surprised him, for in the spring of 1914, she had told him that she was probably going to have a child. But he had expressed some doubts in such a way that she had not insisted, and their relationship had quickly fallen apart.

Why did she keep quiet? Why did she not try to convince him? Apparently she dared not, given Edouard's standing. Moreover, she had perceived in his detachment a sign of fate: she would be an unwed mother, as had been her mother, her maternal grandmother, and two of her aunts. She, too, would raise her child without the help of the father, but with the support of those experienced women. She added that her Parisian girlfriends had very much taken care of her and that her mother had not hesitated to welcome her six month old little girl whom "her goats could abundantly nourish!" So, she had asked nothing of him, if not a little consideration.

Edouard did not at all doubt anything she said. In fact, he immediately wanted to see the child, to discover in her everything that lived in him. He found that he had wanted to be a father for a long time, and Angèle was giving him this opportunity. He proposed to accompany her to Noizay as soon as the circumstances would allow. Meanwhile, they see each other often, and every week he gives her a bit of money for the little one. Mother still does not know anything about it. Her health being as always very precarious, Edouard is waiting to have seen the little one before telling her.

And that, dear Auguste, is all I know for now.

I hope to receive news from you soon, and pray that you and

Marie stay safe and sound. Know also that we are very proud of you![14]

> *Kisses,*
> CLOTILDE

❦

My very dear Eugénie,

What luck and what a pleasure to talk to you on the telephone while stopping by your aunt's house! What a shame that we were interrupted in the middle of our pleasant and reassuring conversation. Let us hope that the telephone lines will be quickly repaired so that you may again converse with your most generous aunt, whom you resemble so much! I also hope that the postal services will be maintained so that you may read these interrupted "news."

I am taking up my story where I left off, that is, the complicated return of Angèle into Edouard's life. So, when he spoke to Mother of their meetings and of the existence of the little girl, she was outraged. She asked him how he, such an intelligent man, could let himself be taken in by that "hussy." He answered that he wanted to act as a good Christian, recognize his faults, and of course, to feel the joy of being a father. That did not mean that he was going to "abandon her, on the contrary." He added that Angèle could be a valuable aide for Mother in view of her state of health. That did not exactly convince her as she fears that Edouard, by engaging himself, will have much less time to give to her. But she did admit that "that girl" might prove herself useful, and that her presence would be a true relief for Edouard and for me.

I must add that Angèle not only offered to take care of Mother when her work would allow it, but also that they did not need to "rush things," as it is never easy for a mother to accept the idea that her son might prefer another woman over her, especially after so many years! That remark proves how much Angèle, far from being greedy, is, on the contrary, generous and devoted. I am thrilled at the idea of welcoming her into our family as a legal wife, as soon as possible. And certainly you can imagine how much Edouard and I are impatient to meet his little daughter, but we must be patient because going to the countryside is not simple, as you well know.

And so, my dear, I hope to tell you more in a short while. In the meantime, take good care of yourself and Pierre, and enjoy to the fullest the presence of your children and grandchildren, now that you are in Limoges very far from Arras and from its oh so murderous front!

I hug you all with affection and ardently pray that these furious battles may rapidly lead to a cease-fire, and then to peace!

Your old Clotilde

༉

MAISONS, OCTOBER 16, 1917

My sweet Eugénie,

I thank you for your condolences and the flowers Madame Riester brought us in your name. Mother would have loved them. They told me how much you would have liked to be by our sides on Saturday, and that we were in your thoughts, early Friday morning . . . You know, as I do, that at moments of great fragility, a simple sign of friendship by your presence or the gift of flowers or prayers touches us profoundly. So thank you, and thank you also for your so constant friendship.

The service took place at Saint-Eloi church, as planned. Our priest gave a nice sermon: "Christ has not come to explain suffering but to fill it with His presence." How beautiful and how powerful! We sang the psalm and the oration of the *Last Goodbye* with emotion and conviction. And during the service, the organist enveloped us in the warm overcoat of Gounod's *Requiem*. It does not have the touch of Gabriel Fauré's, or the amplitude of the grand organ of the Madeleine, but the melodic beauty was there to remind us, even in our sorrow, that our souls find consolation in art and beauty. Yes, these rites give funerals their full significance, and a completely different dimension! We were so small and frail and suddenly we were rebuilt, united, strong and nearly at peace. Obviously, the pain is there, but it is bearable, nearly soothing. This is certainly the why of Faith, its incontestable necessity. Whoever denies this to himself is exposed to the most miserable of lives and the loneliest of deaths.

I was also touched by the number of people who came; in these times of war, I did not expect so many of our colleagues and friends, they who mourn sons, fathers and husbands. I am that much more cognizant in that Edouard and I are losing only an ill and aged mother who could no longer bear to live, and had asked for months to leave this earth for the after life. God heard her prayers; we must accept her departure and thank the Lord on High for his mercy.

We buried our mother in the little cemetery of Bercy that you know so well. I purchased a plot where Edouard and I will go to join her when the time comes. A nice headstone of gray marble will mark the tomb next month. For now, a large ceramic Christ on the cross, and several wreaths and as many bouquets hide the sandy earth piled on the oak casket: a life concluded. All is said.

October is definitely the month of deaths in our family, even though there are also some births . . . But I admit to not thinking of October 1st with much pleasure. Who would want to be 45 already and have so little to expect of tomorrow? My only wish is that the war end: but after three years of intense battles, of lives torn apart, of unimaginable destructions, we can hardly see what could change the catastrophic course of things so soon. Nonetheless, I am going to pray that better days come.

Write to me soon, my Eugenie, tell me that you are all safe in Limoges and that Pierre, thanks to his post, can, in no way, be sent near the front.

Your so grateful Clo who sends you her love

જ

My very dear Friend,

I am thrilled to know that you are all reunited and in good health or almost. And, just like you, I hope that Paul André will not be able to use his broken leg too soon. I imagine in fact, how happy you must be that he is in good hands at the Limoges hospital, and thus, near you, and above all, far from the front for a few more months! Let us hope that the peace, proposed by President Wilson, will be signed before your dear son's return to health. I am optimistic, as the now rare bombardments are no longer such a source of worry in Paris and its environs. Pray God that it continue so and that our soldiers may finally return home.

I wanted to tell you, too, that I often think of Simone these days: I cannot believe that she is already 24 years old: how time passes! So it must be that you are nearly — No, I dare not say it, having crossed that fairly upsetting event almost four months ago! Thus life continues . . . But there are sometimes nice surprises that must be shared to give ourselves hope and satisfaction. I am referring to Edouard.

Yes, perhaps you have guessed: my brother, being a

very responsible man officially recognized his daughter on December 28TH. So now we have a little Jacqueline Loeven in our family. It was for both of us a very moving event, in spite of being limited to a signature at the town hall! I must also add that Edouard and Angèle had spent three days in Touraine, at the beginning of December, to celebrate their daughter's third birthday. Edouard came back deeply moved. He did not expect to be so susceptible to the charms of the little one. I have not seen my brother this happy for years! And in these times of war, the least joy is more than welcome! I do not need to tell you how impatient I am to meet her myself!

She will be legitimized by the marriage of her parents, which will take place in four days! Yes, January 21ST if all goes well . . . I will describe for you the details of the ceremony at town hall in the 12ème arrondissement and in the Church of Saint Eloi. Things will be simple, as imposed by wartime and restrictions. A dozen people will be invited, especially friends and colleagues, since members of our immediate family have disappeared or are far away.

There you have it, my Eugénie, all the news for now. Let us hope that Big Bertha[15] will be forever retired . . .

> *I send big hugs and pray that you stay together, all safe and sound.*
> YOUR CLOTILDE

༄

My very dear Friend,

What a joy to hear you this afternoon! I cannot believe my good luck at being able to telephone you. Your voice has not changed, and I could imagine your smiles during our brief conversation. Moreover, feeling you so close has given me some patience: your coming to Paris in September does not seem so far away.

I can now think again about our short conversation and give you some arguments that I did not have the time to explain, during those three minutes that the operator granted me. Here then is my answer to your question: how do I manage my solitary life without the presence of a loving man? I keep busy with my work and enjoying my music!

Let us speak first of men and of their absence. It is quite simple: from those who claimed to love me so much, to the point of wanting to marry me, not one was truly faithful and involved. They all quickly found another woman after our break-up; only one showed me a solid and durable friendship. I also discovered, over the years, that not one remained faithful to the woman who came after me . . .

It would seem that these men, as devoted as they may be, cannot resist the charms of a newcomer. Are they tempted by the challenge? Do they see seduction as a feat, no matter the pain that they inflict, or who is watching them? And I am not speaking here of flighty or fickle men, but of those who seem so stable in their feelings, yet who, at an unexpected moment, succumb to the temptation of conquest.

And yet, they are so proud of the enduring friendships that have with other men and sometimes a few women. Why do they not think of love in those terms? Why do they not con- struct a relationship that is founded, just as friendship is, on a responsible commitment, a solid fidelity, a deep trust? I feel that the only difference that determines the nature of these two kinds of relationships, apart from the carnal aspect, is that love is supposed to be exclusive whereas friendship is not.

Perhaps I see these things in a naïve, even simplistic way, but in the course of all these years of sentimental adventures, what I have always lacked was trust. So, if one doubts, one can build nothing durable. This "fault" is mine; it has been in me since my childhood. As you know, my father destroyed my trust in men who are supposed to love you and protect you. I have never found one, who has been able to give back to me that trust, that assurance that he will be by my side forever. That explains without a doubt the persistent mistrust that lives in me for 38 long years.

Do not be sad for me since I am surrounded by very true friends — of which you are the best example — and that allows me to live my life as a single woman with vigor and even with spirit. I am in charge of that life, no one controls my activities, no one imposes his views, his desires, his certainties on me.

You might think that I have deprived myself of the happiness of motherhood, but, in fact, would I ever have had that happiness? And what is there to say about the immense suffering of losing a child, as so many women have these last years? That is a tragedy that has given single women (old maids or others) a true acceptance of their "solitude."

I have, furthermore, the joy of having a niece to whom I feel very close. In fact, I know, in my deepest being, that Jacqueline will share, in a few years, my tastes, my expectations. What more could I ask for?

Yes, life has given me much. I am very conscious of it and thus profoundly grateful, whether it be to God or to any other "responsible party" for our destinies.

So, my friend, that is where I am on this sweet and pink evening in May. And you? Tell me about your many activities, your responsibilities as much-loved wife, as cherished and very respected mother, and as indispensable grandmother!

And enjoy the happiness brought by all those dear ones who surround you so tenderly.

Your friend who sends you big hugs.
CLOTILDE

P.S.: I cannot believe that our Simone is already 25 years old and that she is awaiting her second child! For me, she is (and always will be) that adorable little girl with mischievous smiles. Tell her how much I think about her!

✂

MAISONS, JANUARY 5, 1921

Dear Angèle and Edouard,

I just received the beautiful photograph of our sweet Jacqueline. How could I thank you enough? It is the best Christmas gift I could ever receive.

I also appreciate her wearing the dress I made for her sixth birthday. It seems to fit her well. She looks so poised, and older than her age!

As I told you on Christmas Eve, I feel so blessed to share those precious moments with you, and to cherish and pamper our beautiful little girl!

Well, I have to run but will be very happy to come and share your dinner on Saturday.

Many hugs and kisses,

CLO

❧

Dear Cousins,

Just a short note to tell you that no, Edouard is not doing better. He went to the hospital rue de Vaugirard the day before yesterday. They will try to stop the gangrene infection by cutting off his leg a little higher, below the knee. The loss of his foot affected him greatly, what will the loss of his leg do?

For now we remain hopeful: he is a strong man who fights hard. Also, this great hospital is well known for its excellent surgery department; we know the director a little, and he is very reassuring. Of course we pray God with all our might that the infection will stop and Edouard can enjoy many more years with us all.

Angèle is struggling but has not given up her work; what more could she do anyway? It must be said that, for her as for me, work is a welcome diversion since, beyond the anguishing waiting and praying, nothing else could occupy us more efficiently.

We hope to see you in Paris this spring. In the meantime, send us some uplifting news.

YOUR CLOTILDE

ᥱᢥ

PARIS, JUNE 24, 1924

My very dear Cousins,

Our Edouard left us yesterday morning. Angèle and I are heartbroken, disoriented; we cannot believe that he has left us so soon. But it is true that his condition had deteriorated after the amputation of May 31. A serious infection invaded the wound, which could not healed. We had lost all hope.

However, he very much appreciated the visit of his little Jacqueline, last Saturday. I imagine that he was then able to leave without regret. When one has suffered so much, going to God is a great consolation.

It is our turn, now, to accept his departure, and to find a certain consolation in knowing that we will meet again, in a few years, when our time has come.

His funeral will be held Thursday at 11:30 in Saint-Eloi church, and he will join Mother in the Bercy cemetery.

I know that you will be with us in your thoughts.

YOUR CLOTILDE

ᥱᢥ

MAISONS, SEPTEMBER 8, 1925

My dear Eugénie,

I hasten to reply, now that my dear niece has gone back to her mother. I must admit that her presence distracts me so much that I cannot find a minute to do anything but see to her wellbeing. I live a sort of other life when she is with me. In her presence I suddenly discover how much I miss the joy of being a mother! Ah, to shape this little being; show her what life is, show her its pitfalls, its beauty; give her what she needs to find her place and pursue her happiness . . . What meaning that would give to my life!

You asked me to describe her character. At first she can be a little timid, but once we gain her trust, she is everything I never dared to be: impish, enthusiastic, talkative and even a bit of a liar. That does not prevent her from being very observant, with a logical mind that is surprising for her age.

There is also a bit of sadness and a sort of "savagery" in her. In effect, for ten years this little girl had to make due with the care of her grandmother, who was, herself, quite depressed by the death of her son in 1914 and overwhelmed by her daily work, which far exceeded her strength. That woman had a lot of merit, but, apparently, little patience and no leisure to spoil to any extent her grandchild. Of course, Angèle and Edouard went to Noizay as often as possible but, as you have often told me, it is every night, every morning that children need to feel the attention of their parents. It is this attention it seems to me, that she greatly missed.

Losing my own father at the age of ten was heart breaking for me since, up until the end, Papa was attentive and affectionate with me, even when he was overwhelmed by his work or infuriated by others. To this day, I have many regrets. Yet deep within, I believe it must be still more difficult to bear an absence that has no name, a disappearance that leaves you without memory or measure, a sort of melancholy that is persistent and ill-tempered. That is how Jacqueline shows a certain indifference towards this father who did not raise her, nor guide her, nor encourage her. She seems barely more conciliatory with her mother because she missed her as well: since Angèle had to work in Paris while Jacqueline was raised by her grandmother in Noizay. At least, that is the way I see it.

I want so much to repair this injustice (I know that Angèle shares the same need), but how can we undo what fate has imposed on us? For the time being, I am content to spoil her, to show her that she is at the heart of my concerns. Her mother does likewise. But is our little one aware of this? She is often restive, so I do all I can to win her, to retain her, to impress her, for she got the better of me. I am helpless when confronted with her desires and her mood swings. She is a little princess and does not know it. But my Lord, how charming she can be! You, too, would melt! Well, I really need some advice from you, the devoted mother whom life has not spared either.

Tell me where you stand in your project for moving: will you be coming back to Paris soon? Your children and grandchildren would be as happy as I would!

I cannot wait to see you . . . Many hugs and kisses.
CLOTILDE

MAISONS-LAFITTE, NOVEMBER 29, 1926

My dear Angèle,

I thought long and hard about your question concerning the instrument with which Jacqueline could learn to play the music that thrills her.

Yes, our little one is malleable, but solid, and her long hands bespeak a great agility in her fingers. So, you will say, why not the piano? Upon reflection, here are my thoughts: the piano is too masculine for her, too intrusive. Indeed, we attack the music piece, we jolt, we jump left to right. The piano haunts you, bores into you. The piano takes over. Its bursts assault you, exhaust you. Moreover, this instrument is cumbersome, it demands a prominent place in the vast drawing rooms of the pretentious, music-loving bourgeoisie, as you well know.

As a passionate harpist, I am wary of pianos. I am not sure

where this suspicion comes from, but I should explain to you that as an adolescent, I felt that pianos had stolen my father and, no doubt, killed my grandfather! I see your smile, but you must admit that I am not that far from the truth.

To return to our subject, I do not believe that Jacqueline is made for the piano. I might add that it is neither its price nor the high cost of moving it that bothers me: this instrument does not suit her because, my dear Angèle, our little one is all sweetness under her timidity. She would not have the aggressive energy the piano demands, even if she can be impulsive and determined.

No, I think she needs an instrument that is easy to carry, to handle; an instrument that can express her mood, her sensitivity; an instrument that can take her from laughter to tears in two beats three measures, as it were. Do you see where I am going with this? For me the choice is clear: a violin!

Yes, the violin with its contact with the body, the chin; those vibrations that enter and transport the musician: the violin, without any doubt. I can already see her agile fingers flitting from string to string, her firm hand guiding the bow tenderly but firmly, the movement of her chest emphasizing the movement of her wrist, the sweep of the chords . . .

You undoubtedly understand my enthusiasm, so I will stop. But tell me quickly if you two agree with me, and I will immediately start looking for a well-made instrument, with character but without pretension. I have in mind a violin from Laberte or Couesnon; it will not be difficult to find and it will be a nice Christmas gift for Jacqueline; a gift I will offer her when you come to Paris in December.

I hope I have convinced and even delighted you both with this idea. Write me soon to assure me that I have.

Affectionately yours,
CLOTILDE

P.S.: The small package I sent to Jacqueline yesterday, should arrive just in time for her birthday — I hope . . .

✑

MAISONS, TUESDAY, NOVEMBER 8, 1927

My dear Angèle,

I hope you are all doing well and getting ready to celebrate the anniversary of the Armistice: nine years already! And yet, we are still not consoled over our losses: I think of you, of your mother in particular, of your Georges René. I think also, of course, of our sweet cousin Jean-Paul d'Argis, whom you met and admired for his kindness, his wit, and his retorts. He, too, gone, at just twenty years of age, as so many others who have left us, far too soon. My God, how all those men are missed!

But we have to keep an outlook that is more positive, more optimistic to be able to celebrate life. Yes, you know what I am talking about since the arrival of your nephew, little René, last September, has given all three of you the happiness that was so cruelly taken away in 1914. So give all my best wishes for good health to the little man, as well as to your sister. I hope to meet him and to see her again upon my coming to Touraine, next month, which is a real delight for me, as you know.

That leads me to tell you again from where I get that optimism that surprises you sometime: Jacqueline, my adorable niece. You know how attached I am to her, how I find pleasure in coddling her, how she has quite simply given a real meaning to my life. And for that, my dear Angèle, I am for ever indebted and deeply thankful to you.

You say that she enjoys my letters and especially my post cards. She has assured me, in fact, that her collection "grows under her very eyes" — which makes me very happy, since for me it is a great pleasure to send them to her!

It is clear that happiness depends most often on very small things: peach jam for example! Yes, I must tell you how much I enjoy the one you brought me in September. I am not a very good cook, but I will catch up to you with my knitting, if that is fine with you.

> *With much love, my dear Angèle, and the joy*
> *to see you soon*
> CLOTILDE

℘

SUNDAY, JANUARY 15, 1928

My very dear Jacquot,

If only you knew how much pleasure I have reading your nice letters, you would write me day and night! However, I have not received the one that you say you wrote between Christmas and January 1ST. Did you put your address on the outside?

My darling, even though I have not been able to finish your little dress, I promise that you will have it before the end of the month. Until then, please continue to tell me, in detail, of your pleasant and studious life. I do not doubt that you will receive your diploma with no difficulties next July.

Do you know that our new chapel is dedicated to Sainte Thérèse? You told me that you really like her. So I chose this little postcard to please you. Write to me soon, my little Jacqueline, to tell me if I am right.

> *Your aunt who sends big hugs,*
> CLO

℘

MAISONS-LAFITTE, JUNE 9, 1928

My darling little Niece,

You may rest assured that your sweet letter, received last Monday, gave me the most pleasure! I was very impressed by all the details you gave me about the visit to the exposition of Art Nouveau works that you saw in Tours. You seem to have captured the emotion that one feels in front of these beautiful paintings. And I know that these landscapes will inspire you when you, too, try to paint or draw them.

I am also quite pleased that you very much liked the other works of art and that you understand better the artistic processes. I think this visit will strengthen your abilities — let us say rather your talent — and your love of drawing and watercolor.

Furthermore, your style is progressing: I see that you like to study and that you pay attention to everything that you are taught. Keep going on this path, as it will lead you to success in school and beyond!

I was also happy to learn that you are all doing well and that you enjoy fishing for nice trout in the Loire with your parents. I am sure they must have been delicious in the butter sauce that your mother makes so well!

I await your next letter with great impatience, and send many tender kisses,

        Your auntie who loves you so much
        CLOTILDE

☙

MAISONS, JULY 12, 1929

My dear Angèle,

Thank you so much for your letter that arrived two days ago and I am thrilled with your good news. I am sure that your

145

mother appreciates being in Basses Rivières, so near to you while still maintaining a certain autonomy. She, who was so active, would, indeed, find it hard to completely depend on her daughters, even if she is about to celebrate her 73RD birthday!

I am happy that you have fully recovered from your erysipelas; that disease is one of the most painful. It is understandable that you still feel fatigued after a month of fighting it and worrying, so do not apologize. Moreover, I am not surprised to learn that our Jacqueline took her role as nurse very seriously. She learned from you when it comes to taking care of her family. You gave so much of yourself during Edouard's long illness; I will never forget your wonderful devotion to my brother!

I have also not forgotten my dear niece's desire to continue her art studies. As soon as she has her diploma in hand (which I do not doubt, given her motivation) and if you agree, I will arrange her entry in the Julian Academy. It is an excellent institution that will enable her to enter the Beaux-Arts School in Paris well-prepared. Jacqueline already shows real talent, but she needs to work hard and acquire a solid foundation in order to succeed in such a difficult career. You will say that all that costs too much, but I am ready to give her the necessary financial support. What is more, she should be able to easily obtain a scholarship as a Ward of the Nation.[16] So let me know what you think and do not hesitate to let me contribute!

Those are, my dear Angèle, my thoughts right now. I pray that you all stay in good health and that our Jacqueline remain disciplined and motivated in her studies.

I pray also for our good Auguste. Have you heard of him recently? It may be that he and Marie are separating. After sixteen years of living together, it would be a pity, but such is life: we never know what it has in store for us.

I take comfort thinking often about you, and would so much

like to see you. Will you perhaps be coming to Paris during the summer? If not, I could go down to Blois at the end of August. Meanwhile, I wish you good health and send hugs to you and to Jacqueline.

Please also send my best wishes to your dear mother and to Mr Lejeune.

CLOTILDE

PARIS, AUGUST 31, 1929

MAISONS, NOVEMBER 8, 1929

My dear Niece,

How are you? I hope you are well in spite of that aunt who is making you wait too long for that promised little jacket. And now it will be even a bit later, because I lost a sleeve on the train where I had planned to work on it. Of course I had to order some more wool that should arrive in a few days.

So, my dearest, while waiting for that warm piece, I thought I would offer you a lighter one, white and brown, that I will send right after this letter. You can wear this little vest between your dress and your coat. The other, the warmer one, will follow soon.

You will find also in the package a book that should please you: *Tales of the Woodcock* by Guy de Maupassant. I found it quite interesting and fun to read.

Now, do you forgive me? Say "yes," and I send you a big kiss. Give your mother a big hug for me.

Your auntie who loves her Jaco,

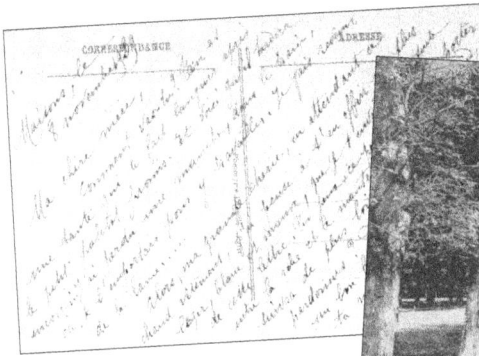

CLOTILDE

MAISONS,
NOVEMBER 22, 1929

PARIS, JANUARY 8, 1930

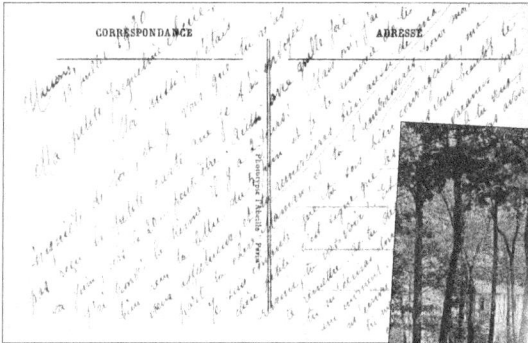

MAISONS, JULY 19, 1930

FRIDAY, AUGUST 15, 1930

My dear little Jac,

When I think that it has been eight days already since I was
with you, and how much fun it was to tease you, I would like
to do it again today!

I have not yet framed your nice watercolor, but it is on my bedroom wall, held in place by thumbtacks, and it speaks to me of you. It will find its final spot at the end of next week, I promise!

On my way to work this morning, I thought about our lovely walk with your mother in the vineyards and of how much I enjoyed it, although it was already the day of my departure — how quickly good times pass!

And you, are you resting some? Do you take walks with the same enthusiasm? I do not stop thinking of you and pray that everything will turn out for the best in the coming weeks. Take advantage of your readings, and tell me what you think of Victor Hugo's works that you are now reading. They should both inspire you and develop your vocabulary.

I am always thinking of you, and send big hugs,

Your auntie who loves her "baby,"

Clo

⌘

MAISONS, DECEMBER 18, 1930

My dearest little Jacqueline,

I came home a little early tonight, so I will take advantage of this extra time to write you. Did you receive the letter and the little package that I sent for you birthday? 16 years old already! I cannot believe that you have already reached that "advanced" age of a young woman!

150

But you must be very busy doing your end of the year homework, unless you are actually writing to give me some news — as it happened several times already: "our" great minds think alike!

Will you stay in Rochecorbon on the 24TH, or will your mother bring you to Paris? Tell me soon so that I know where to send your little Christmas present. If you come to see me, I will be very happy to give it to you personally and to chat with you about the things we love, as you may imagine!

My dearest little Jaco, I pray for you and your mother. Hug her affectionately for me.

I hold you in my heart and hope to see you soon,

Your auntie who loves you so much,

CLOTILDE

MAISONS, DECEMBER 28, 1930

My dear little Jacqueline,

You know that you always give me the greatest pleasure when you talk at length about yourself in your sweet letters. Of course I have even more pleasure when you are with me. So, ma Chérie, imagine my disappointment when I learned that you could not come this week, and that I would not be able to hug you for a long time to come!

I was hoping we could go together and buy a little gift for you to celebrate Christmas and the New Year. Instead I am sending a little money order with this card. Upon receiving it, go to Tours and buy

yourself something you really want. And tell me all about it in your next letter. If you still have a little money left, you could put in your savings account.

Had I already chosen something for you, I would have put it in the little suitcase that is awaiting you. You will take it when you come to Paris, as it may not be empty . . .

My sweet Line, give your mother a hug from me, as big as the one I am sending you from deep in my heart.

Your aunt who loves you so,
CLOTILDE

ↇ

WEDNESDAY, JULY 22, 1931

My little Darling,

Your pretty letter just arrived with your wonderful news! Bravo, bravo my Jaco! So now you are in possession of the *brevet elémentaire*,[17] and ready to continue your studies at the Ecole Supérieure in Tours; I am so proud of you! And I do not doubt that your parents are as proud of you as am I!

I am thrilled to welcome you next month at Maisons-Lafitte, and I have started a list of things that we will do together. At the top is the Colonial Exposition about which everyone around me is saying the most wonderful things.

I am also going to keep my promise and make a few small changes on the little summer dress that awaits you. I think you will like it very much.

A thousand big kisses from your auntie,
CLOTILDE

ↇ

MAISONS-LAFITTE, JULY 28, 1931

My dear Angèle,

A thousand thank-yous for your letter and the good news concerning your mother's recovery: I am very pleased as all of you are!

As for our Jacqueline, she will go far! Since she obtain her Elementary Certificate so easily, she will have no difficulty passing the Superior Certificate that will open a nice teaching career, which you have been wishing for a long time. Perhaps she can also teach Drawing beside French, in a secondary school.

I am also thrilled about your coming to Paris mid-August; and of course I will welcome Jaco with the greatest pleasure, while you visit the daughters of Mr. Lejeune. I intend to take her to the Colonial Exposition and to the Louvre, as well as to a concert in Maisons-Lafitte; what do you think of these options? We will talk about all of that when you arrive.

Until very soon then, I send you big affectionate hugs,
CLOTILDE

༺༻

MAISONS, MONDAY, SEPTEMBER 15, 1931

Dear Cousins,

Your last letter was two months ago; did you not receive mine around August 10TH? I am a bit worried about you, but I do hope that you are in good health and happy. Tell me what is happening in St. Omer during this fairly cold end of the summer, and after the torrential rains of last month. I must say that in spite of the often cool weather in Pas-de-Calais, I envy your country life full of calm and gentleness. But Parisian I am, and Parisian I shall remain! Even though

Maisons-Lafitte is not exactly Paris: one breathes better here and Gentlemen are more gallant!

But I do have something new to tell you. Let me begin by saying that the Bataille Company having closed, I had to find another "career." I am now a typist at Dormsel. Imagine me, striking away with speed and precision on the Remington with a French keyboard: letters, ribbons, reams and papers no longer have any secrets for me. And my training as a harpist affords me many advantages over those typists with no musical training! Hence, in spite of my age, my fingers and wrists do not tire as quickly as do theirs. So I have acquired a certain status in our office . . . Still, the softness of silk and the play of colors are sorely missed. Well, we have to adapt and accept the changes that life requires of us. Now that my wrist had regained all its flexibility, I play the harp and draw every evening at home, which gives me great pleasure.

My niece and my sister-in-law are doing well. Angèle often asks about you; seven years already since you have seen each other! You undoubtedly know that she moved in with a former colleague who had retired a short while after Edouard's passing. They seem to get along very well and enjoy being in Touraine, between their rabbits and their garden. She also takes care of her mother, Mrs. Schmit, whom you met at Edouard's funeral, as she lives near them.

Jacqueline is becoming a very accomplished young woman. I am enclosing a portrait taken last spring, so that you might see how much she takes after the family! She wants to teach visual arts and is studying for the entrance exam at the Ecole Supérieure in Tours. Aunt Emilie and Uncle Louis would be happy to know that a great-greatniece shares their passion and will devote herself, just as they did, to the education of children. We all pray for her success.

I also had the pleasure of welcoming her to my home at the end of August, and of taking her to the Colonial Exhibition, in the company of Robert Banisso, the young Dahomeyen adopted by our cousins the Valmorins. He is a charming boy whom Jacqueline much enjoyed. Just as you, we were much impressed by this exhibition, in many respects. We will talk about it more when you come in Paris this winter.

As for the Valmorins, Jeanne now runs a boarding house on Valette Street. It is a good solution for her since Robert helps her while he pursues his studies. Still, she has not grown accustomed to her widowhood: she was telling me last Monday that she sees Pierre everywhere, in the street, in the metro. She has not yet accepted his passing; and she also misses Guadeloupe. It is clear to me that as we age, we need to reconnect with the people and the places from our childhood!

But I must close in order to go to a friend's house. I await a nice letter from you, filled with news and stories about your life of luxury! Actually what is happening to the Bouchers d'Argis? I have not heard any news from them for several months.

Your very affectionate,
CLOTILDE

୧୬

My dear Auguste,

Following our conversation Sunday evening, I would like to give you some details on my impression concerning the colonial exhibition; an impression that may perhaps surprise you, given my limited knowledge of those far away lands. At first, just like you, we much admired the constructions, the costumes, the colors, the smells of the exotic dishes, and so many other things. The American singer-dancer, Josephine Baker (whom you so enjoy) was really touching, and we do not doubt that her new song "I Have Two Loves" will be a hit around the world, just as you told me with such certainty!

Of course, Jacqueline and Robert are constantly humming it.

But let us get back to the exhibition: little by little, during the visit, a bizarre feeling, mixed with sadness and suspicion came over me. You see, those natives taken out of their world did not seem happy to me, in spite of what the guide to the exhibition said. You must also have noticed that they were all busy doing what they were supposed to show us, but in fact they looked tired; they kept their eyes lowered, hardly ever smiled, and were not saying a word to each other. It felt like I was at a silent movie but with no wit or laughter! My malaise grew even more as we were leaving, when Robert told us that life in Africa, and in Dahomey in particular, was very different from what was depicted. This very superficial presentation of African cultures had totally erased the negative side of colonization! I must admit that I now share his point of view. What do you think about it, you who have known all those countries and lived in Havana for several years?

Jacqueline really enjoyed the event and could not stop asking questions which I could hardly answer. She had to be content with Robert's slightly sarcastic answers. I do not know if she actually learned anything from the visit, but I do hope she will cultivate this bubbling curiosity that makes her so charming, and that she will be able to keep an open mind.

On the good side of things, do you know that Albert Laprade's handsome building at Porte Dorée is going to become a permanent museum? We expect its inauguration at the beginning of November, upon the closing of the exhibition. It will house the most remarkable works of primitive art assembled during our conquests. A "temple" to the glory of the peoples who today make up our "Great France," as the Minister of Colonies would say! You cannot stop progress!
So those are my thoughts, my dear Auguste, on that subject.

I eagerly await speaking again with you about this exhibition because you always have very interesting ideas about this kind of event.

I would also like to know what your young friend thought about it, in order to know her a little better, to understand her, or really, basically to understand your decision to devote your life to her.

I must say that since your separation, I miss Marie a lot because we shared so many things: our love for the arts and fashion in particular. I also appreciated her rebellious spirit accompanied by a remarkable empathy toward the less fortunate. But I also understand how you were seduced by a woman much younger than yourself: it makes you feel younger (and at 56, who would not like that chance?). I suppose also that your conquest was a sort of challenge. Are you thinking to make her your wife in the near future?

I will stop these indiscreet questions and let you savor your new life with Madeleine, who must certainly enjoy the way you spoil her!

> *Till soon,*
> *Your overly curious cousin,*
> CLO

♋

Miss Jaco,[18]

Tell me, does this landscape, photographed this way, make you think that it is far from Paris? That shows us how the photographer's choice of viewpoint, the angle from which he considers the scene, is essential. The reaper at rest is barely visible, and his scythe with the white blade could be the wing of a heron if you do not notice the handle against the tree trunk, which underlines the transparency and size of the lake.

A beautiful work, really, and a post-card of this part of the Bois de Boulogne that ought to please my dearest Jacqueline.

Your auntie,

CLOTILDE

SUNDAY, JULY 17, 1932

My dear Eugénie,

It has been too long since I have written to you. Thus it is from my hotel room in Blois that I break this silence that should not have happened.

But before I tell you my news, you should know that I learned yesterday from your cousin Pauline that your leg was getting better and you were planning a quick trip to Paris, as soon as you are able to go up and down the stairs in the stations and the treacherous steps of the trains. I pray to God that you feel courageous enough to spend a few days in Maisons-Lafitte. As you know, the house has not moved; I am still five minutes from the station, and there are only four steps to climb to enter my house.

So, I am in Blois, at the Hotel de France as usual. Such memories . . . ! Jacqueline is astonished at the brightness of the rooms, the bathroom, and the salon walls covered with velvet. Me, I see mostly that memorable evening that we had been waiting for, and which changed our plans so unexpectedly. What would your life have been if we had stayed away and not joined in that frantic dance? If you had not gone and placed yourself between that tall, handsome Jean Lacoste, who would not stop making eyes at you, and his persistent, friend, Jean-Louis? How could we have thought that a little friendliness would have no consequences? How could we have been so naive? Once we recovered our reserve, how could we not have guessed that it would only whet their interest, their appetite? Should we regret now your brief engagement and my long relationship, your evenings with neither silence nor rest, and mine so often solitary? I cannot imagine another course, but even if I could, it would not take me very far, since the path of our fate is not in our hands.

Little does it matter, as I think I have found an alternative to nostalgia: I want to teach Jacqueline about the dangers that life will not fail to place in her path. Her mother is doing the same, but it takes more than two or even four to protect our girls, as you yourself have told me often. I must say that, just as we did, our 17-year-old Jacqueline listens to us with a half-serious, half-dreamy attitude, but she keeps her own opinions. She has enough imagination to understand the dangers, but too much assurance to fear them. Just like us, all of us! What goes around comes around. So, should we worry that much? Should we give up, or share with her our hopes in spite of our fears? I take it on myself to give her a positive vision of life in the hope that she will keep her interests high. I want to motivate her, nourish her ambitions; but will she believe me? I fluctuate endlessly between optimism and apprehension.

Nonetheless, our little meetings in Blois are a delight for me, and I believe that she, too, enjoys the beauty of these moments spent together. The elegance of the place, the serenity of the river banks, our love for sweet delicacy satisfied, thanks to the pastry shop in rue Denis Papin: all of these pleasures are trump cards in my hand. I wish she would love me as much as I love her, but I know it cannot be the case: she has so much charm, and I so little. And she already has a mother . . . No, what she needs is her father. Monsieur Lejeune cannot, ever, take his place. And yet Jacqueline never speaks of Edouard, she does not seem at all curious as if she had completely forgotten him. I speak to her of our family, but she is mostly interested in the grandparents, whom she never knew and thus does not miss.

On the other hand, she loves to hear me speak of my childhood, of the life in Paris, of painters and concerts. We also speak a lot about fashion and dressmaking. We carry on a perfectly natural conversation between a curious adolescent and the aunt who cares so much for her. But she often seems aloof. In fact she is the princess and I am simply one of her subjects. To maintain my place I have to pay her court. That is as it should be.

So there we are, my dear Eugenie, these bittersweet reflections that my time in Blois with this child too much loved evokes. Now I understand your complaints of a mother so often frustrated by the distance your daughters aim at putting between you to show their independence. Is that a new fashion? Were we so tied to our mothers, so aware of our duties and of their needs? Are the short skirts and boyish haircuts just some signs of this fundamental change?

I notice that this letter is full of questions. It is because I miss so much your insight, your understanding of others.

161

Come soon to visit me so that we can talk about this
and finally understand and accept the true causes of our
frustrations, our little mishaps, but also our great fortune to
have those adorable and much-loved children so close to us.

With much love,

YOUR OLD CLOTILDE

ε⅄

PARIS, MARCH 15, 1933

My dear Angèle,

I hope you are all in good health and eager to take a little
trip to Paris. I am looking forward to seeing you since I am
now installed in my new apartment at: 9 rue de la Vieuville,
Paris 18ème.

As you know, I am on the second floor. My windows open
on the street. One nice bedroom, a large living room and a tiny
kitchen are plenty for me. The little couch in the living room
can easily accommodate one person, so Jacqueline could stay
with me while you go visit Mr. Lejeune's daughters.

The neighborhood is quiet and the subway station is near by,
on the Place des Abbesses. It is the deepest station in Paris as
you probably know (since it was opened in 1912), but there is
an elevator, so you do not need to worry. If it is out of service
for some reason, you get off at the Pigalle station and walk up
the rue Houdon. It is not very far. Also, it takes less than an
hour to get to my place from Porte de Charenton. Needless to
say how much I appreciate our metro and all the new lines that
are being built little by little!

I am still quite surprised to find myself in a tiny Parisian
apartment after my life "in the country." I had forgotten the
black walls and the dust, the constant noise of wagons, the
glaziers[19] shouting and the street urchins screaming; it is almost

the rue de la Forge Royale, without the noise of saws and the smell of varnish. Life goes on in cycles!

The best aspect of this is the proximity to my workplace: no more risk of missing a train, no long streets to walk in snow or rain, no more warnings for involuntary tardiness; and the transport savings are significant — you know how it is!

As for the grave, my dear Angele, do not worry. I go there often and have no problem maintaining it. The little primroses that you put there last month are in full bloom and brighten up the periphery of the marble headstone. It will soon be nine years since Edouard left us; I still cannot get used to his departure, and this return to Paris renews the memories of the years spent at his side. I felt so close to him, he was such an affectionate, and attentive brother. I pray for him often, for my mother, and also for my father: though I still do not know where he is buried, in spite of your advice and my research.

But let us think rather of the living, the young, and allow me to inquire after my dear little niece. I have not had any news from her for two weeks. I imagine she is busy with her studies: exams are coming! I think of her often and hope she will have great success again this year.

> *I hug you both, as well as your mother,*
> *with great affection,*
> CLO

PARIS, JULY 13, 1934

My dear Line,

I will write at length only after your exams, so you can keep your full attention on your revisions. Write me as soon as it is all behind you.

But I want you to know that every day, for more than two

months now, I send you a big kiss in my thoughts . . . often several! And these coming few days, there will be many more! I await with impatience, your good, reassuring news, and pray for you, for your success!

I will send you next week the book by André Malraux, *La Condition Humaine,* which received the Goncourt prize last winter. You can read it after your exam. It should inspire you. I, for one, really liked it. We will talk about it during my visit at the end of August.

Give your mother and your grandmother big hugs from me.

A thousand kisses and wishes from your auntie
who loves you so,
CLOTILDE

⁂

FRIDAY, SEPTEMBER 29, 1934

My dear Jacot,

I share your deep disappointment and your sorrow, because you had worked so hard to obtain your diploma. But do not be ashamed, for those who receive it are few and far between! Moreover, in spite of this defeat, your mother and I much admire your efforts and your courage. The qualities that you have shown are still in you and you will know to use them when necessary.

You must also consider that you have not, until now, much appreciated your work as a substitute teacher in the village of Parçay Meslay. You will now be able to work more and with pleasure for the photographers of Tours and its region.

You shall know as well that each destiny is unknowable and that what we hope for is often not what we receive, but that makes us stronger and more determined: your mother and I have known setbacks and still managed to take advantage of them. You share our resilience so you will know how to go ahead while waiting for "the man of your dreams."

I hope that this short letter will lift your spirits a little, and I send you many big hugs.

> *Your Auntie who loves you so much,*
> Clo

❧

PARIS, NOVEMBER 7, 1936

My very dear Friend,

Yes, my letters are becoming rarer, but I do not cease thinking of you, of all those who surround you, of those little ones who give you such joy. So why not pick up my pen more often to share my joys, my thoughts with you? When I think about it, I see two different reasons that are, nonetheless, contradictory.

The first is based on the magical invention, the telephone. You know the pleasure it gives me each time I hear your voice, that I discover again the vivacity of our conversations: the distance disappears. Although I cannot see your affectionate smile, your eyes full of malice, your soft hands in mine, all of that rises in me during those few minutes thanks to your voice . . . But our calls are so short and we have so much to say to each other, that they leave me hungry for more. Well, you will say, that is a good reason to write! But no, because the second reason of my "silences" intervenes. It is a simple reason: I have very little to say, to share! A life of routine, days limited to work that is not demanding, exchanges full of banalities with my colleagues, a weariness that keeps me from going to the Paris of art and music. Add to that the disappearance of those who gave us so much: friends, parents,

165

cousins . . . And of course the distance that separates me from you, from Jacqueline, from Auguste. What is more, I do not even see those who live in Paris, for in the evening I am too weary to leave my nest!

This "reason" is in fact a state of the soul based on an absence of enthusiasm and the feeling of having arrived at the stage of life where there is no longer room for engaging projects, and where the past "chases off" the future.

So, my friend there you have my not very pleasant explanations on what concerns me. But do not cry for my fate, because I also live some very good moments! Your letters, your calls (on the telephone), your profound friendship give me many such moments! And there is Jacqueline, her letters and little visits! And finally there is still and always my harp that calms me and reassures me each evening in spite of the fatigue in my fingers and my wrists; a fatigue due to that typewriter that monopolizes me all day long . . .

Upon rereading this saddening letter, I wonder if it would be better to put it in the trash (to use office language). But, in fact, I must send it to you since our promise, so often renewed, is to share everything. In addition, I now feel lighter and ready to "get out of my hole!"

Thank you, thank you my friend for having given me, once again, the opportunity to open myself to you and to lift that weight from my shoulders.

Your Clo who tenderly hugs you and waits
impatiently to "give you a ring."

(That expression is so funny to me, since I cannot give you a ring as you are already married and we are both women!)

My dear Eugénie,

Your letter, received on the 2ND, made me laugh so hard!
And I am thrilled that your Pierre has kept so much wit in
spite of his age! Yes, to know how to make others laugh is a
good thing, a talent that we should retain and even revere!
Laughter is one of the rare and great pleasures that old age
does not steal from us. And what is more, little funny stories
help us capture and retain the attention of the youngsters who
surround us, especially if we have no other good means of
drawing that attention. So, my friend, tell your dear husband
that nothing could give me more pleasure that his puns and his
hilarious remarks!

Now let us get to your questions concerning Jacqueline's
marriage. First of all, and you are correct, they became
engaged in December, a short while after their first meeting,
just like you! And Jean is not exactly Jacqueline's first love:
three or four years ago she had fallen for a young neighbor, a
teacher, who seemed very interested. But last year he married
"out of duty" another girl, who was also a former student
of the Ecole Supérieure in Tours. Jacqueline was crushed
but refrained from speaking about it. Should I see pride or
common sense there? Both, perhaps.

Here is a succinct report of the marriage, which was
wonderful. You will also soon receive the photo taken by Tours'
excellent photographer, for whom Jacqueline has been doing
touch-ups for the last four or five years. She will not have to
do any this time, so perfect were they as a couple, and of an
elegance that one rarely sees in the countryside.

Jean is an extremely charming young man who comes from
a simple but warm family, as are the people from Touraine. His
father, who works in insurance, gave a speech, both interesting

and witty, that showed his generous soul. His uncle and witness, Louis, showed a lively wit that kept all of us laughing. Mrs. Goujon is very proud of her son, and she seems to fully approve of her son's choice by being very accommodating toward her young daughter-in-law. Nonetheless, it was the groom's sister, Simone Besnard, who, with sweetness and deftness, was able to draw Jacqueline from her timidity in order to give her the place she deserves in this new family. In short, Angèle can rest assured and hold her head high: her daughter is "well married" and happy.

The family went by automobile clear to the town hall of Rochecorbon. It appears that all of Jean's friends, being shopkeepers, have one. There was a crowd at the Central Square! The mayor was very courteous and eloquent it was clear that he held our young bride in high esteem. The procession to the church was quite a charming spectacle with two young children (nephew and niece of Jean) throwing rose petals on the pavement before them. Still I have one great regret: Edouard was not there to lead his daughter to the altar. He would have been so proud of her! Thank God, Jacqueline did not seem saddened by his absence: the past is not yet part of her concerns for she has her future to conquer, to shape!

The church was full of magnificent flowers; the sung mass particularly beautiful: Mrs. Schmit and I had done our best to have it thus. Although Angèle and Jacqueline would have been happy with just a quick benediction, we wanted everyone present to have the time to be filled by the importance of the moment. And we succeeded: the religious ceremony gave rise to much emotion and tears.

I think that afterwards all the town's inhabitants were at the church doors to wish the newly-weds well and to express their admiration. I must say that Jacqueline, Queen of May these last two years, had a court of admirers among the Rochecorbon people: a fair return if we think of the scorn that she suffered in her childhood in Noizay and Vernou.

A beautiful reception followed at the Lantern restaurant on the quai de la Loire. Delicious plates; great wines, some bottles dating back to 1921, surprisingly sweet; and a magnificent wedding cake. One eats decidedly well in Touraine. During dinner, according to the custom, everyone sang or recounted stories to honor the newly-weds. The most beautiful moment was assuredly Telemann's *Fantasy in B Minor* played on the flute by Jean's cousin, René Bezault, who is first prize winner in Rome. I was quite surprised by the interest that such a piece caused among the guests, who counted few musicians. I might add that this *Fantasy* is full of verve and can inspire a public accustomed to jigs and other music in the old country tradition. Next, René played a fantasy from *Carmen* that unleashed the guests' enthusiasm as they began to sing all together: Bizet would have been thrilled to see that his work was so appreciated!

Of course the young people danced a lot, to the great pleasure of the elderly parents and relatives who, seated about the room, did not tire of reliving their own youth while watching them, even though the dances themselves have greatly changed!

That is my report for tonight. I hope it has amused you. I go back to Paris tomorrow, and will send news of our lovebirds when they return from their honeymoon. They chose a grand tour through the Midi, passing through Geneva, Nice, Toulon, and then the Atlantic coast. They are not planning to go by Artois, which will be for another trip, according to my niece.

Take good care of yourself and of your Pierre, my dear friend.

> *Lots of big, big hugs,*
> CLO

❧

PARIS, NOVEMBER 16, 1938

My dear Friend,

I am taking advantage of my lunch hour to share some wonderful news with you: Jacqueline gave birth on October 31 to an adorable little girl, first names Janie Claude Juliette. She was born at her grandparents' home in Château Renault because Jean and Jacqueline had gone down to Touraine to attend the marriage of one of Jean's cousins. The baby's arrival was a bit unexpected, as the doctors had said that she should be born another ten days or so later. But the birth was easy and the little family was able to return to Paris on the 11TH.

I am so happy to be a great-aunt since I cannot be a grandmother! You understand my enthusiasm, you who have already twice had such happiness.

Still I worry about Jacqueline for she has already gone back to work at the bar and kitchen; it's a heavy job, although Jean had the good idea of hiring a young neighbor to help in the kitchen and take care of the baby. The girl is full of good will and is eager to please Jacqueline, whom she considers a role model. It may also be that Mrs. Schmit, the grandmother of whom I have often spoken, will come up to Paris to help our little family, now that Angèle and her partner have left Touraine to move to Montargis less distant from Paris where all their children live.

I hope to send you a photo of my niece and her little one as soon as possible. In the meantime, enjoy your own children and their adorable families. Oh, Eugénie, thinking of you, of your Simone, of Jacqueline, and now this little Janie, reassures me and chases away those so sad thoughts that come from the newspapers: the wildfires near Marseilles and then the massacres and destruction everywhere in Germany. We are so lucky not to be confronted by all that and to be able to count on those young people who love us and give us so much joy.

I leave you now to take up my work again, but you remain ever present in my thoughts, waiting for your arrival in a few weeks.

> *Your friend who send big hugs,*
> CLO

જ

PARIS, AUGUST 20, 1941

My dear Angèle,

It is with a heavy heart that I send this little letter, as a kind of announcement. Yes, alas, our Auguste passed Monday evening resulting from a wound he received on the 15TH of this month while repairing his automobile. The wound was very deep and became infected so fast that nothing could save him.

We celebrated his 66TH birthday just three weeks ago. I

cannot get used to the idea that he is gone. He was like a little brother, all grown up, upon whom I could count come what may, and that was even before losing Edouard! I thought him invincible for, ready to face anything, he was able to find unexpected solutions in any circumstances.

His young wife, Madeleine, is of course well provided for, at least for now. But in these times of war, nothing is certain. Let us hope that she, like you, will face this terrible loss with courage and determination. Moreover, what deeply saddens me is that he leaves behind a 10-year-old boy who will never benefit from the gifts of his father: his intelligence, his wit, his generosity. Yes, it is very hard to accept his unexpected departure. But I have to admit that he led a most interesting life and was able to serve those he loved with devotion.

I want to believe that he has found peace and even happiness in the hereafter that awaits us and about which he spoke with great humor since his mother's death, some twenty years ago! They are reunited now, they too, and not just in the tomb in Montrouge cemetery that you know well.

In spite of my pain, I think often of you and hope that you are doing well, all three of you, in Montargis, in spite of the bombardments and the high cost of living in every sense of the word! Jacqueline shares with me your news each week when she brings some very necessary food, which I much appreciate. Furthermore, her visits are a true joy since she comes accompanied by your adorable grand-daughters. I delight in their charm, their sweetness and thus forget for a bit those difficult moments in life. Nothing can lessen my pleasure of sharing those moments with them!

As you surely know, because of a persistent edema, my health is becoming precarious. But I pray each day in the hope of seeing you in Paris in a not too distant future, in spite of the German occupation.

> *Affectionately,*
> Clotilde

๛

My very dear Friend, (Louis Renault)

Forgive this long silence due to the fact that I had so little to say to you outside of my admiration for your hard work and vigilance. We are going once again through a period of uncertainty, a period often terrifying. I wonder how you can go forward, knowing that each one of your decisions might cause a catastrophe, not only for you and your loved ones, but for all your employees and the entire nation. I feel sorry for you, just as much as I admire you.

But you already know all that. If I am writing to you today, it is not that I expect an answer from you; it is simply a way for me to feel less lonely. A serious case of edema is causing me to suffer cruelly and preventing me from going out. What is more, I do not really know to whom I can turn to find some moral support. My little Jacqueline is taken up with her work — Jean has been called for duty — not to mention her two little daughters, as well as the constant problem of finding food. My sister-in-law and my cousins the d'Argis are too far away to visit me more than once a year. August being gone, his second wife does not show much interest in our family. In short, I am stuck here within my four walls and am counting on our friendship to keep me company for a little while.

I think back on our youth, our discoveries, our follies,

and I laugh, happily. All these memories warm my heart and, for a few moments, I forget how the latter has trouble beating regularly. The noise of the footsteps of the German patrol beneath my window invokes the memory of you, so resplendent in your uniform on August 2ND 1914 . . . I see you again squinting, your finger raised as if to tell us that you will certainly find a way to meet and combat the enemy on your own ground. For you, every problem had a solution; every crisis was merely an opportunity to go forward. Where did you get this unbelievable, priceless strength that caused so much envy?

This strength, that warms me once more, is nonetheless my only regret. Yes, today I can admit it to you: I would have loved so much, for once, one little moment, to be of use to you, to be the one you needed! You, more than anyone, because I have so much affection for you . . . But once more it would not be. It pains me to say that God willed it this way: on the edge of the grave, it happens that the greatest believers suddenly doubt the divine and His design. But I digress. Forgive me this excess of weakness, and know that writing to you has given me the strength to face tomorrow, if such is my destiny.

I thank you for being such a faithful friend, and I hug you with all the tenderness that neither time nor distance can suppress.

Yours forever

CLOTILDE

P.S.: Excuse my terrible handwriting: my swollen hands are having trouble holding this beautiful Waterman pen that you gave me for my birthday, almost 20 years ago already . . . Do you remember?

My so dear Eugénie,

I know that this letter will not reach you, but it will join the other drafts carefully kept in my notebooks, as I often follow the advice of Sister Thérèse, "in order to measure our epistolary progress." Those drafts remind me of all those events that we have lived and the emotions felt along our many years of friendship. They are, in a way, the ties that link us to our past, to our existence. A true source of reflection.

But what should this letter, undoubtedly the last one, tell you? Simply, that I need to share with you, with your soul which is there, perched on my shoulder like a laughing bird, these thoughts that have been in me for months. Fairly agreeable thoughts, for I think myself very lucky, for many reasons. You see, I was so loved! I was able to count on the infallible support of my family, my friends, of which you are foremost.

Moreover, I was luckily able to appreciate the beauty that surrounds us, nourishes us, brings us together. Thanks to that beauty, in its multiple forms, my long life was filled with exciting discoveries, precious, exalting moments. I want to believe that my artistic and other activities were useful and even appreciated by those with whom I shared them. Furthermore, I enjoy the great pleasure of having passed to Jacqueline my love of drawing, of color, of fabrics — if not of music. I think I also reinforced her independence of mind, her determination as well as her respect for others and her compassion toward those who suffer. Thus my "raison d'être" (although unmarried and without children) is no longer in question.

These thoughts are not so very different from those that you expressed before you left us. Your Simone admits to finding a true consolation each time she recalls your last exchanges. Will mine have that beneficial power? I doubt so a little, since I have not often the opportunity to share them, as you well know! Jacqueline's weekly visits do not lend themselves to philosophical discussions, since she often comes accompanied by her adorable little girls. Angèle is too far away and Madeleine lives in Senlis, since the passing of our dear Auguste; so we have hardly any contact. In the end, with my worsening health problems, I had to take a leave of absence last week: hence this silence, this solitude. A solitude that leads to reflection and to the pleasure of writing to you despite uncooperative fingers.

What to tell you of my failing health? The edema, which is spreading, will take me to the hospital in a few days, according to my doctor. I would prefer to stay at home because it is clear that I will not outlast this sad winter. It does not matter because my departure will not be a great sadness for anyone. In these desolate times, so many are suffering far more than we can imagine! No, my little aches and pains do not compare to the suffering that ravages our country. And I will add that dying, at my age, does not frighten me; if this tired body wants to find rest, I must let it do so.

Furthermore, as you know, dying does not mean disappearing, it is starting an adventure of which we know nothing. This departure is the beginning of something else, a discovery made of encounters, of rejoining! It is neither the end, nor nothingness, it is the apotheosis: it is quite simply what we call paradise! That is where I will find again all those whom I miss so much, you in particular!

It is a shame that in this world where fear reigns, where compassion and forgiveness seem inaccessible, so few people accept the idea of a beyond, of an afterlife . . . I pray that around me everyone finds that calming peace, source of well-being, of felicity.

And so my friend, writing all of that to YOU has done me a lot of good. I am also going to caress my harp, who is bored, alone in her corner for at least two weeks . . .

I eagerly await seeing you again in the company of Emma Calvé who left this earth almost two weeks ago according to the *Petit Parisien,* but whose voice still sings in my ears, which does me so much good!

Your Clotilde at peace, thanks to you . . .

CLOTILDE died at the Vaugirard hospital on February 13, 1942, ten days after her arrival. She had the pleasure of seeing Louis and Jacqueline again before falling into a comatose sleep on the evening of the sixth day. She rests in the Bercy cemetery, as she announced in 1917, near her mother and her brother. She has received visits from her grand-nieces every spring for the last fifty years, and is delighted — according to the blackbirds who nest in the tree shading the tomb, and who peck at the basket of petunias flowering faithfully on the marble slab.

Endnotes

1 The *fouriéristes* were the followers of Charles Fourrier who believed in the necessity to build an open and liberated society based on Saint-Simon's ideology.

2 The French nobility was based on two dedications: the military (*noblesse d'épée:* nobility of the sword) and the government (*noblesse de robe:* nobility of the gown).

3 Location of the Mesureurs' apartment where the little concert in question took place.

4 Refers to Florian's fable about the monkey who fails to light its lantern, the origin of the French expression: "éclairer ta lanterne."

5 Before the 20TH century, a rooster was placed atop the steeple of all village churches, not simply to indicate wind direction, but to remind the villagers that a brighter, Christian future was coming.

6 The catastrophic fire that destroyed the Charity Bazaar on May 4.

7 Refers to the Siege of Paris during the Franco-Prussian War of 1870–71.

8 The French official driver's license in use before 1922.

9 Charlus's song "Le chauffeur d'automobile" was very popular, from 1899 to 1920, but the use of slang and the mentioning of body parts made it unacceptable and embarrassing for ladies and young women.

10 A street on the west side of Paris where the Boucher d'Argis, Clotilde's cousins, live.

11 Julie D'Aiglemont is the main character of Balzac's novel: *La Femme de Trente Ans* (*A Woman of Thirty*).

12 Clotilde wrote this short sentence in English, which explains the postscript.

13 Compagnie du chemin de fer Métropolitain de Paris: the Parisian metro company that became RATP in 1948.

14 Auguste was working for the secret service of the French army in London.

15 A powerful Germany canon built to destroy the fortifications along the French borders in 1918, named for the daughter of the Krup Company's owner.

16 A child whose father, military or police officer, died while in service.

17 Le brevet élémentaire (Elementary certificate) was the diploma obtained after passing an examination at the end of the 10TH grade. It was required in order to enter the Ecole supérieure where one could pursue two more years to obtain *le Brevet supérieur,* the elementary school teacher's certificate.

18 Clotilde enjoys using *Miss* rather than *Mademoiselle,* to remind Jacqueline that speaking English is fashionable among educated women.

19 Glaziers would walk all day long through the streets, shouting to hawk their talents and wares.

Renowned people and companies mentioned in the Letters

Aubert, Louis (1877–1968): singer, composer and soloist in the Madeleine church choir.

Auclert, Hubertine (1848–1914): journalist, author, suffragette who fought hard for women's rights.

Bataille, Companie: fabric manufacturer well known for its colored cotton fabric.

Bernhardt, Sarah (1844–1923): artist, comedian and a businesswoman who owned her own theater in Paris, Place du Chatelet.

Bizet, Georges (1838–1875): pianist, French composer of operas, *Carmen*, *The Pearl Fishers*, *Symphony in C major*, among others.

Blanchet, Maison: fabric wholesaler, located in Argenteuil (a suburb of Paris).

Bonnard, Pierre (1867–1947): French painter, illustrator, engraver and sculptor. One of the founders of the Nabi movement, he exhibited his work at the *Salon des Indépendants*, each year.

Boucher d'Argis, Comte de Guillerville, Jules Gaspard (1814–1882): Squadron leader in the Cuirassiers regiment, then writer, speaker at the Caen Academy. Caroline Guyot's husband, father of Alphonse, Jules, Henri and Paul Louis; Clotilde's great-uncle.

Calvé, Emma (1858–1942): very famous singer, soprano who sang at the Paris Comic Opera, Milan La Scala, the Royal House of London, the New York Metropolitan Opera, among others.

Carnot, Sadi (1837–1894): statesman, President of the French Republic, assassinated in 1894.

Caron, Rose (1857–1930): cantatrice, music teacher, soprano famous for her performances in operas by Wagner, Reyer, Verdi and Gluck, among others.

Chambefort, Maria (1840–1893): photographer, specialist of daguerreotypes, located in Roanne (Loire department) where she opened the very first photography studio.

"Charlus" stage name of Louis Napoléon Defer (1860–1951): a very popular French singer at the turn of the century.

Cheret, Jules (1836–1932): painter and lithographer whose renowned posters influenced artists such as Seurat and Bonnard, and stimulated the development of the publicity industry.

Clovis, Frank king (466–511); he converted to Christianity in 496, under the influence by his wife, Queen Clotilde.

Couesnon, Maison: musical instrument manufacturer, very famous between 1882 and 1960.

Crawford, Francis Marion (1854–1909): American writer born in Italy where he lived for 30 years. He published many novels, short stories and successful plays: *Francesca da Rimini* in 1902, among others.

Dellaleau, Ernest (1827–1864): painter from the Pas-de-Calais region; second husband of Emilie Guyot, the great-aunt of Clotilde.

Durand, Marguerite (1864–1936): actress, journalist and suffragette. She founded *La Fronde* newspaper after working for *Le Figaro*. She played an important role in the French women's movement, and their voting right in particular.

Enfantin, Prosper (1796 –1864): graduate of the famous Paris *École Polytechnique*; socialist philanthropist and entrepreneur.

Fauré, Gabriel (1848–1924): organist, composer, teacher, choir master at the Madeleine Church and director of the Paris Conservatoire.

Florian, Jean-Pierre Claris de (1755–1794): poet, novelist, fabulist; member of the French Academy.

Fourier, Charles (1772–1837): philosopher, founder of the Fourierist movement.

Furnion: silk manufacturer, supplier of the Parisian fashion designers, the "Grands Couturiers".

Gérôme, Jean-Léon (1824–1904): painter, president of the Beaux-Arts Academy in 1895.

Gouges, Olympe de, pseudonym of Marie, née Gouze (1748–1793): femme du monde and writer very engaged in the fight for women's right and against slavery. The Montagnard government sent her to the scaffold as she opposed its violence during the French Revolution.

Gounod, Charles (1818–1893): pianist, prolific composer of operas and church music.

Grasset, Eugène (1845–1917): designer, decorator, engraver of Swiss origin, who played an important role in the Art Nouveau movement.

Gréville, Henry, nom de plume of the writer Alice Marie Céleste Durand née Fleury (1842–1902): Prolific author whose works appeared in the *Revue des Deux Mondes, Le Figaro, la Nouvelle Revue, le Journal des Débats*, etc. with considerable success.

Laberte, Maison: violin maker founded around 1780 in Mirécourt (Vosges). Those luthiers' violins had an excellent reputation between 1880 and 1940 given their quality and affordable prices.

Lameire, Charles Joseph (1873–1956): decorator, painter who worked on many Parisian churches.

Launey, Charles de, nom de plume of Delphine de Girardin née Gay (1804–1855); writer, essayist, playright and poet who published chronicles in the newspaper *La Presse* on the history of Paris. She welcomed in her salon the most prominent writers including Balzac, Gauthier, Musset, Hugo, Dumas and George Sand.

Leghait, Louise, née Reynders (1821–1874): renowned Belgian photographer; first woman member of the French Society of photography.

Léo, André, nom de plume of Victoire Léodile Béra (1824–1900): novelist, journalist engaged in the fight for the rights and the education of women and workers. Socialist, she actively supported the separation of church and state years before it took place, in 1905.

Léon, Pauline (1768–1838): wife of Théophile Leclerc and founder of the Société des Citoyennes Républicaines Révolutionnaires in 1793. She fought to obtain from the government a more active role for women, but she was seen as too leftist and did not reach her goals. She returned to her work as a chocolatier in Paris and then in Vendée, to feed her family.

Le Soufaché, Joseph-Michel (1804–1887): architect who worked on renovating castles such as Versailles, and built several mansions for aristocrats in Paris.

Lesueur, Daniel, nom de plume of Jeanne Loiseau (1854–1921): poet, novelist, translator, playwright, literary critique for several newspapers, journalist for *La Fronde* and *Femina*.

Mesureur, Gustave (1847–1925): political figure; French Secretary of Commerce in 1895. His wife, Amélie, née Wailly (1853–1926) was a writer and poet. Suzanne (1882–1927), their daughter, was an excellent violinist who became a well respected composer.

Michel, Louise (1830–1905): teacher, speaker, journalist and anarchist activist who dedicated her life to the defense of women's rights and women workers' needs in particular. She participated actively in the Paris Commune in 1871 and was deported for nine years in Nouméa. She continued her libertarian activism until her death.

Montagne, Pierre de la (1832–1907): contractor, builder of important projects in Paris.

Mucha, Alphonse (1860–1939): Czech painter, illustrator and decorator who lived in Paris for 20 years. He worked for the publisher Armand Collin, and for Sarah Bernhardt, designing her theater posters.

Nadar, Ernestine née Lefèvre (1836–1909): photographer, spouse of the famous French photographer Félix Tournachon known as Nadar.

Parrot, Philippe (1831–1894): painter from the South of France, whose remarkable portraits placed him among the best artists of his time.

Phillips, Stephen (1864–1915): British poet and playwright whose works were very successful, notably *Paolo and Francesca* in 1900.

Pissarro, Camille (1830–1903): a Danish-French Impressionist painter, student of Courbet and Corot. Close friend of Seurat and Signac, he guided and inspired Renoir as well as the Post-Impressionists Cézanne, Gauguin and van Gogh.

Pizan, Christine de (1364–1431): Italian-French woman of letters born in Venice, who was able to live by her pen in medieval time. She ardently fought for women's rights and the need to educate young girls. Thanks to her talent of poet and writer, she gathered the support of King Charles V and many contemporary thinkers.

Renault, Alfred (1928–1892): draper, husband of Berthe (1842–1917), father of Fernand (1865–1909), Marcel (1872–1903) and Louis (1877–1942) who opened the car factory bearing their name. The Renaults were neighbors and friends of Clotilde's cousins, the Boucher d'Argis de Guillerville.

Roger & Gallet: founders, in 1862, of the perfume company bearing their names.

Rouyer, Louis (1819–1905): artist and art professor, friend of Ernest Dellaleau, husband of Emilie Guyot; Clotilde's grand-uncle.

Saint-Saëns, Camille (1835–1921): French musician, organist, and composer.

Saint-Simon, Henri de (1720–1825): philosopher, writer, creator of the socialist ideology.

Sand, George (1804–1876): née Armantine Aurore Dupin, wife of Casimir Dudevant. Prolific writer who influenced deeply the French society of the time, in the areas of politics, literature and social iniquities: women's rights in particular.

Scudéry, Madeleine (1607–1701): a woman of letters, creator of the "roman à clef" who impressed her contemporary readers. She welcomed in her literary salon the renowned thinkers and writers of her time: La Rochefoucault, Mme de Sévignée, Mme de La Fayette, among others.

Sévignée, Madame de (1626–1690): author of *The Letters*, which describes the life of the French aristocracy of her time. Considered essential to grasp French culture, *The Letters* have been taught in every French secondary school since 1881.

Singer, Isaac (1811–1875): American builder of sewing machines.

Stern, Daniel, nom de plume of Marie d'Agoult née Marie Catherine de Flavigny (1805–1876): writer, essayist. Even though she belonged to the French nobility, she welcomed many republican activists in her salon.

Telemann, Georg Philipp (1681–1767): German composer and Chapel master.

Thomas, Ambroise (1811–1896): Organist, composer and president of the Conservatoire de Paris.

Tristan, Flora, wife Chazal (1803–1844): writer, essayist, socialist activist, friend of Charles Fourier, she proposed some ways to improve the lives of factory workers and the condition of women all over the world.

Trouillet, Angelina (1831–1881): photographer specialized in children portraits.

Van Hartmann, Karl Eduard (1842–1906) German writer and philosopher, author of *Philosophy of the Unconscious*.

Acknowledgments

I AM deeply grateful to all of those who so generously sustained me during the realization of this complex and challenging undertaking.

I am particularly indebted to Françoise Saunier and Alain Minczeles for their help with the French version; to Jim, my husband for his participation in the translation; to Nancy Gil for the final English version, as well as her meticulous corrections of both the French and English texts; and to Miguel Gil for his enhancement of the photographs.

I will not forget Mireille Miné, Erin and Coco Haenlin, Yvane Bouillard and Ken Larson for their countless encouragements.

Many thanks of course to Anne Kilgore for her patience and talents, concerning the design of the book.

www.ingramcontent.com/pod-product-compliance
Lightning Source LLC
Chambersburg PA
CBHW031255090426
42742CB00007B/470